COGNITIVE BEHAVIORAL THERAPY

A Step-by-Step Guide to Overcoming Anxiety and Rewiring Your Brain to Regain Self-Esteem and Control Over Your Emotions

Daniel Cloud

CONTENTS

To my beloved wife

Who always supported me

To my children, the guiding light of my life

Prologue

Cognitive Behavioral Therapy (CBT) is a research-based treatment approach for mood and anxiety disorders that combines both cognitive and behavioral methods. It has strong support in the scientific literature as an effective treatment for depression, anxiety, eating disorders, and other conditions. The central proposition of CBT is that situations are analyzed through cognitive frameworks that lead to specific thoughts. These thoughts lead to feelings that can be pleasant or unpleasant; in the case of anxiety and mood disorders, therapy usually addresses uncomfortable feelings of distress, fear, or hopelessness. Since emotions are often difficult to change directly, CBT focuses on changing the thoughts and behaviors that lead to these feelings. Its premise is simple: By being mindful about your thoughts, you can control your feelings and, consequently, your actions.

Psychologists Albert Ellis and Aaron T. Beck developed CBT back in the 1950s. Dr. Ellis had initially been a proponent of classical psychoanalysis but lost faith in the method over time. Influenced by ancient and modern philosophy, especially Stoicism, Ellis created a new form of therapy that focused on helping patients understand their own irrational beliefs and restructure those that lead to emotional pain and suffering. This approach is known as Rational Emotive Behavioral Therapy (REBT) and bears many similarities to CBT.

Dr. Aaron Beck helped conduct research to support this new concept of "cognitive therapy." He is usually considered the "father" of cognitive behavioral therapy, which combines the cognitive restructuring elements with behavioral modification. He also explained how dysfunctional thinking could lead to psychological problems. After being a supporter of classical psychoanalytic theories, he began looking for new approaches when his experiments were unable to validate those concepts.

This method of cognitive therapy is completely different from older models of psychoanalysis. Psychoanalysts did little to engage their patients, who had a mostly passive role. Often, attention was focused on discovering the root of the problem and did not necessarily change thought patterns or behavior to counter it. Cognitive behavioral therapists avoid this approach.

When working with a patient, CBT-based therapists aim to help build a set of skills that can be developed, practiced, and applied outside the therapy sessions. This aspect, which may include readings and at-home exercises, makes CBT different from other therapies that focus on discussing problems and offering advice during visits. These skills include having an awareness of thoughts and emotions and being able to identify how different situations influence thoughts and behaviors, how thoughts and behaviors effect emotions, and ultimately, how dysfunctional thoughts and behaviors can be modified in ways that lead to more pleasant and manageable feelings.

Cognitive Behavioral Therapy is a form of psychotherapeutic treatment that focuses on the feelings and thoughts that influence behavioral patterns in patients. It is used as effective treatment for different disorders like addiction, anxiety, and phobias. Through the treatment process, the patient learns how to identify thought patterns and how to take control and change them, especially those that have a negative impact on your emotions or behavior patterns. CBT focuses on helping those who need it learn to develop an awareness about their thoughts and the way it shapes the world around them.

The main purpose of the therapy is to help people change the way they think and look at everything around them. The moment they do, their entire world begins to shift.

CHAPTER 1: Cognitive Behavioral Therapy: A brief introduction

This therapy was created in the 1960s by psychiatrist Aaron Temkin Beck. At the time, Beck was conducting psychoanalysis and observed during these sessions that his patients were inclined to have internal dialogues in their minds. However, they reported only a small fraction of this thinking to him.

The thoughts that the patients went through would make them feel a variety of negative emotions from anxiety, fear, annoyance, and sadness. After a series of research and tests, Beck concluded that there was a link between feelings and thoughts, and this was unexplored territory in human thinking and behavior. Knowing that this was a significant relationship, Beck coined the word 'Automatic Thoughts' to explain the thoughts filled in emotions that automatically pop in people's minds every now and then.

Beck's research found that humans didn't always know of these thoughts, but they have learned to identify somehow and report them. Many of us are not aware of plenty of the things we do and say but when it comes to negative interactions and scenarios, our minds tend to exaggerate our thinking to the point where it creates more issues and problems.

Beck called this cognitive therapy because this correlation had an importance in the way we thought. In modern medicine, it is known as cognitive-behavioral therapy, because of the importance of techniques for behavior techniques as well.

CBT has been tried and tested under many successful trials scientifically in many locations and by different groups. CBT has been tested in a wide range of problems, and while cognitive and behavioral elements are different from the therapies used, it all comes under the umbrella of CBT.

CBT borrows from the concept that your feelings and thoughts define your behavior. A good example is if you spend most of the time thinking about and worrying about air disasters, you will find it difficult to appreciate or even attempt air travel.

With CBT, you will learn that while it might not be possible to control the things that happen in your environment, or influence the stimuli around you, you have the power to control how you interpret them and, therefore, deal with them. Most of the time, patients struggle because they feel they are not in control of their feelings or thoughts.

Compared to most forms of therapy, CBT is affordable, and this is one reason it is increasingly becoming a preferable mode of treatment for mental health experts and other professionals. Cognitive Behavior Therapy, otherwise known as CBT for short, is an approach that is designed to treat a range of emotional and mental health issues. These include treating depression and anxiety.

This therapy is used to address and treat several psychological-related issues, which include:

- Low self-esteem
- Hypochondria
- Insomnia
- Anxiety
- Anxiety disorders (including obsessive-compulsive disorder, social phobia, or post-traumatic stress disorder)
- Depression
- Eating disorders
- Irrational fears
- Substance abuse (smoking, drugs, alcohol, drinking)
- Specific behavioral or emotional problems that children and teenagers may be dealing with.

Over the last 40-years or so, research has only strengthened the effectiveness of this therapy. The main premise behind this approach is to raise awareness that the problems we face in our lives are a consequence of the way we have learned to think and behave. The existing way we feel is a result of the conditioning (what we have been brought up to believe) and previous experiences that have a hand in shaping our perceptions. Advocates of this therapy believe that by changing the way we think, we can have a more positive impact on our emotional wellbeing.

The letter "C" in CBT stands for cognition, referring to the way we think, the mental images that swim around in our mind, our core beliefs, self-talk we engage in, the influence of others, and our immediate external environment. The problem occurs when our thoughts start to develop a "threatening" aspect to them. The more significant and more threatening these thoughts seem to become, the worse we begin to feel. When our thoughts lead us to believe that there is no point doing anything and we're destined to fail anyway, our emotions steadily decline from misery to depression. Those who strongly believe in these unhelpful thoughts have the hardest time breaking out of the cycle of negativity.

We go through hundreds if not thousands of thoughts in a day. Some of them are nothing more than a random stream of consciousness, a way our creative mind expresses itself. It is the unhelp thoughts that linger that pose the biggest problem. What we pay attention to will influence the way we think. If we pay attention more attention to the negativity that is going on, we interpret these experiences as our reality. Catastrophizing, obsessing, blowing things out of proportion, overthinking, overgeneralizing are some of the many ways our thoughts can get the best of us. They become so prominent in our minds that we lose sight of the fact they are nothing more than thoughts, not reality.

The letter "B" in CBT stands focuses on the behavioral aspect and is based on the theory of learning. A perfect example to illustrate the power of learned behavior would be Pavlov's experiment. The Pavlovian Conditioning is a learning process that was first explored by Ivan Pavlov and his team of researchers in 1927 through tests conducted with dogs. Pavlov believed that behavior could be learned through conditioning where a stimulus is administered, and a response follows. His most famous experiment of this theory was when he conditioned dogs to start salivating at the sound of the bell in anticipation of food. The food acted as a conditioned stimulus, and salivation is the response. Today, classical conditioning is a widely known necessary learning process.

Likewise, this therapy is based on the same premise that our emotional responses can be conditioned too. If someone was bitten by a dog as a child, that experience might have led them to develop a fear of dogs. The CBT therapist they work with is going to speculate that the phobia and anxiety that is felt each time they see a dog is a classically conditioned response, even if the dog is friendly and has no clear intention of causing any harm. Using the CBT approach, the individual trying to overcome their phobia of dogs will be exposed repeatedly to dogs that do not intend to bite them. Alarming as it may seem at first, the repetitive experience will eventually help them learn that not all dogs are dangerous until one day, the fear response finally stops being triggered. Repeated exposure to the object or situation you fear most is part of the therapy. Maybe it's not the most pleasant part, but facing your fears and knowing you can overcome them is the only way to heal. Your therapist is going to work with you through these steps, so you'll never have to feel like you're doing this alone.

Our instinct may be to run and hide from our triggers, but avoidance and denial will rob you of the opportunity to build your confidence and strengthen your mental and emotional capabilities. Problems are not going to go away, no matter how much you try to sweep them under the rug and pretend they don't exist. Your anxieties and fears are real, and they need to be dealt with head-on. That is the only solution that is going to work in the long-term.

Finally, the letter "T" in CBT talks about your therapist. The person who is there to assist you and help you better understand why you've developed the phobias, fears, or triggers you have. To understand why you find yourself trapped in this vicious cycle with seemingly no way out. Your therapist is here to guide you as you enhance your knowledge about thought patterns and the way they shape your reality and how to break out of the bad habits that you trapped in this mindset. Here is what you can expect from a competent therapist:

They will understand how difficult this process is going to be for you mentally and emotionally, and they will proceed with genuine empathy, warmth, and positive reinforcement every step of the way.

They focus on building a bond of trust with you as you work together over the next few sessions. They make you feel comfortable, safe, and reinforce that trust, so you feel happy enough to let your guard down.

They work on efficiently maximizing the time that they have with you so you can get the most out of each session. Every session, they will be keen to know what goal you would like to accomplish and work with you to make it happen.

They measure progress and change based on your perspective. A good therapist will not rely on their own judgment because they are aware, they might not always be right. They track success based on how well you progress.

They will teach you to relate in different ways to the various thoughts you have. They will give you guidance on how to recognize your negative thoughts and then challenge them by generating helpful and realistic solutions.

They consistently encourage you to apply your skills in between sessions and follow up with how you progressed. They focus on hearing your feedback and incorporate that knowledge into the next few lessons moving forward, so you're continually improving and never stagnant.

Benefits and Drawbacks of Cognitive Behavioral Therapy

For CBT to be successful, the individual must take an enthusiastic approach. Below, we will be discussing the benefits and drawbacks of choosing CBT to battle your anxiety disorder.

Benefits of CBT

1. Studies have found research that shows that cognitive-behavioral therapy is as effective as medication when it comes to treating anxiety disorders and other mental health disorders.

2. CBT is time-sensitive - it can be completed in a short amount of time compared with other types of behavioral therapies.

3. CBT is highly structured, which means that it can be used in different formats. This includes self-help books, groups, and computer programs.

4. During CBT, you learn skills that are helpful and practical that you can incorporate into your daily life. This can help you cope with current stresses and future difficulties as well.

Drawbacks of CBT

1. In order to fully benefit from CBT, you need to have a commitment to the process. A therapist can be there to help and advise, but they cannot help solve your problems without your cooperation.

2. The structured nature of CBT may not be suitable for people suffering from learning disabilities or more complex mental health problems.

3. Some people argue that CBT only helps with current problems and specific issues; it fails to address the possibility of underlying causes of mental health issues.

4. CBT often focuses on the individual's ability to change their thoughts, feelings, and behaviors but does not address a wider set of problems when it comes to systems or families. These problems typically have a big impact on somebody's health and wellbeing.

In conclusion, CBT is effective when it comes to helping you manage problems such as anxiety, to make it less likely for it to impact your life negatively. However, there is always a risk that the feelings you associate with your problems will return, but if you understand and know how to use your CBT skills, it should be easy for you to control them. If you are practicing CBT with a therapist or through a program, it is important to practice your learned skills even when the sessions are over.

CHAPTER 2: Determining your goals

It is difficult to set goals when you don't know yourself or what your real problem is, but once you've gone through these points, you'll have a clear and honest picture of who you really are and, hopefully, a good idea of how you'd like to change. So, what is it about you that needs to be adjusted so that your behavioral patterns can become more positive?

When it comes to developing your goals, use these points to help you. Don't just think about what you'd like to do. Our behavior can only change when our thinking changes. So, think in terms of how you want to adjust your life and how you feel about different things.

While the words of those close to you may weigh on your mind, you must think in terms of what you want to achieve. This is your life, and the goals must be yours. If you are reflecting someone else's wants and desires, you will quickly lose interest, and before long, you'll give up.

The goals you set will be the basis for each session you have, and it will serve as the foundation for a plan that will help you change your thought processes and behavior. Throughout the rest of this program, you will refer to your goal list several times a week, make adjustments, and as long as you follow through, you will see modest changes take effect very quickly.

How to replace poor coping strategies with more effective ones

Many things can cause depression and anxiety. Circumstances that are beyond our control can take away our feeling of autonomy, that feeling that we are not in control and that we don't have the freedom to make our own choices. There are three things that we must have in our lives to give us satisfaction: autonomy, connections, and abilities. When these things are prominent in our lives, we are happier and have a greater sense of fulfillment. When they are absent, negative feelings begin to appear. We feel ashamed though we've done nothing wrong, we feel depressed, and if we don't have those connections our psychological mind craves, loneliness sets in.

Many who seek out CBT often complain about similar feelings. They are usually in high-stress situations, they do not feel recognized or appreciated for the things they do and are often isolated from those people they truly want in their lives. When that happens, their energy levels begin to drop, and the mental, emotional, and spiritual side of them starts to starve. This is the point when changing behavior is crucial to healing the whole person. It's time to focus on the positive response needed in order to set things right.

You might be wondering if these negative behaviors are triggered by our thoughts. Why exactly do we even need to focus on action in therapy? This is a logical question and certainly deserves discussion. First, getting people to do things they enjoy is far simpler than getting them to change their viewpoints.

Another critical fact to consider is that it instantly addresses those innate needs we all have. By making small adjustments in behavior, such as getting people to do things they thoroughly enjoy, we can get the brain to produce endorphins and trigger an antidepressant effect.

Besides all of that, it can work on our inner thoughts and help dispel some of the negative thinking that our minds are stuck in. This aspect of therapy is referred to as 'behavioral activation' and focuses on changing your actions to do something more positive.

At this point, you've simply identified that you feel anxious and depressed. You may not know exactly what makes you feel this way, but it is unimportant. The key component here is that you have to start doing things that give you enjoyment and pull yourself out of the rut you're in.

The reason for this is because there could be a thousand things buried deep in your psyche that could trigger depression, but it's your response to this negative feeling that is causing the behavior. It is normal for a depressed person to isolate himself or herself, almost as if they were punishing themselves for feeling emotions. They don't speak to their friends or family, they stop doing the things they enjoy, and they fail to find purpose in anything that they do.

We've already determined that both depression and anxiety are standard aspects of life, so what makes us depressed today may not be the same thing tomorrow. We need to teach ourselves the proper way to respond to these negative events when they occur. When we do things that infuse us with positive energy, things slowly begin to change.

When it comes to choosing positive activities that will instill good feelings, they can't be activities that someone else believes is important for you. This is why answering the questions above is crucial to understand which activities will work best. They must be based on your personal goals and what you see as vital to building yourself up. If the activities are prescribed based on your therapist's views or those of someone close to you, it is possible they will work for a little while, but you'll eventually fall back into your depressive state again.

For that reason, you are the only person who is capable of creating this plan of action. Take your time with this as it must be based on the things that you think are the most important to you and will give you that sense of purpose, value, and worthiness.

Short-term vs. long-term rewards

Even though doing things we enjoy is more comfortable, for someone who is dealing with anxiety and depression, it can be quite a challenge. It is simple to write down on a piece of paper that you want to spend more time with family and friends, but it is another thing to break the negative cycle you're in.

If you choose short-term rewards, you'll feel good for an evening, perhaps even a day, but it wouldn't get you any closer to your goals. Later, you'll feel even worse because you knew you really wanted to go out with your friends anyway. So, how do we learn how to choose long-term goals over the short-term ones? We can try some basic strategies:

- Go back to your list of goals you created and choose which ones you value the most.
- Create a list of activities that support those values.
- Make a plan to incorporate those activities into your routine. It could look something like this: "I value living in a beautiful home."
- Clean my living room so I'll feel comfortable having people over.
- Get my decorating kit and add some color to my house.

You may reach a point where you actually complete the positive activities you have on your list, but there should never be a point where you actually meet your values 100%. Values will always have something that you need to work on, whereas activities are the actions that you do to satisfy your values. It's a good idea to create a list of those things that you consider to be important in your life. Again, for everyone it is different, so when you create this list, think only of the things that you think are important and make you feel good.

It doesn't really matter what your values are; at this point, your focus should be on creating a list of activities that will help you fortify these values in your mind. It's quite possible that you won't be able to complete your list of values in a single sitting, and as you go through your days, you will likely think of more to add to your list.

When it comes down to the activities you want to do, you can list them in order of importance. The activities that are more important should be placed at the top of your list, while those that are the least important, even though they give you a certain level of enjoyment, can be put further down on your list.

Once your list is done, it's time to start making these activities a priority in your life. If you've already listed them in order of importance, then you know what actions you need to do first. However, you can take another approach to accomplish this. You could order it based on the level of difficulty, from the easiest to hardest. This will help with getting things done quickly to boost your confidence level and make you more emboldened to tackle those activities that you think are more difficult.

Regardless of which approach you take, you won't be able to tackle it all at the same time. CBT is a progressive approach to negative behavior. By starting with those tasks that won't require special effort to accomplish, you reinforce your mental and spiritual self so that, in time, the more strenuous activities will feel like they are within reach.

Consider obstacles

Before you start jumping in and trying to do things, realize that you're going to face obstacles along the way. Our mind is infamous for playing tricks on us, especially when we're stuck in a negative thought process. If your goal is to have family and friends over, your mind will inevitably start throwing up negative curveballs. "They don't want to spend time with me, they're too busy. They have more important things they care about. They live too far away." All of these negative thoughts present an obstacle that could be thrown in your path. It helps to prepare for these negativities before you even start.

Once you start, you'll begin building up momentum towards more positive behavior, and anyone of these negative thoughts is like an oil slick on a race track. Develop a plan to get around them before you begin. You don't want to ignore these obstacles when they come up, but you want to have a plan to address them when they appear. Otherwise, your life could start spinning completely out of control.

Another strategy you can apply is to give yourself a reward when you accomplish each activity. This is very important when you're trying to complete activities which are more important than enjoyable. Cleaning your house for having friends over is not usually a pleasurable activity to keep you motivated, but a reward will give you a certain level of satisfaction to make it worthwhile.

Make a schedule

It is also important that you give yourself a time limit to accomplish these activities. Since the activities go against your natural instinct to be negative, if you don't have a specific time frame in which to complete them, you are very likely to fall into the habit of procrastination. The idea that you can put it off until later can be an easy trap to fall into.

Create accountability

If you've been in a depressive state for a long time, you're probably not accustomed to having another person held accountable for the things you do. But these activities will pose a challenge for you, and if you allow your negative thinking to get in the way, it will be easy just to dismiss them unless you have someone or something that you have to answer to.

Accountability could be anything from telling someone what your goals and activities are, to keeping a journal detailing what you expect to do, when, and how you're going to do it. If you're responsible enough to make yourself accountable, then keeping a daily diary or a journal may be enough to keep you pushing in the right direction, but if it's not, find a buddy. This could be your spouse, your parents, or your coworker, so you have someone to answer to if you don't complete your tasks.

What are the Basic Principles of CBT treatment?

We have discussed what CBT is already, but what are the basic principles? Well, in order to understand this, we need to think about the different concepts. Cognitive Behavioral Therapy is a type of psychotherapy that helps you change your automatic thought patterns, cope with your emotions, and challenge your negative behaviors. Has anyone ever told you that your actions have consequences? Well, they do! The way we react can stop us from moving on our lives, and that is why it is so important.

To understand the basic principles of Cognitive Behavioral Therapy it is mandatory to explain the nature of its name.

"Cognitive" because the whole idea of CBT focuses on our ideas, beliefs, and thoughts and generally how we feel.

"Behavioral" because the behavior is something we do or the way we act. Sometimes this can be driven by how we feel or our emotions.

"Therapy" because if we are in therapy, we are receiving treatment for some illness we have in order to fix this problem.

Think about an occasion when you have been reactionary. Maybe this is because someone takes something for you or treats you badly. We can be reactionary as our thoughts or behaviors are automatic, and as a result as we struggle to control our gut-reaction. This means we can't always help the way we feel or act, so we get emotional and behave without thinking. This is because we are programmed to think or react in a negative way instantly.

These basic principles indicate how this therapy is focused on what you think and how you act in relation to an event or trauma. They are like a gut-reaction as we respond without thinking. Our thoughts and behaviors occur regularly, but what are automatic or intrusive thoughts and how can we change them?

Cognitive Behavioral Therapy is a well-known psychotherapy treatment that is notable for its positive results and feedbacks. It has helped thousands of individuals overcome different things and helps them regain control in their lives. It caters to different aspects on how a person responds to a certain situation or problem.

CBT is quite a complex and intricate method to understand. It is composed of several different aspects that should be understood before initiating the process. The three main parts of CBT are: thoughts, emotions and behaviors. These are all interconnected and can significantly impact one another.

Starting with the chain, thoughts are one of the most crucial and important aspect wherein if negative thoughts are present, it may lead to negative emotions that can also trigger negative behavior. With that being said, everything lies within what the individual's train of thought is and how they deal with it.

Emotions are also crucial since this greatly indicates what and how a person might feel. Behavior deals with how a person interprets their thoughts and emotions and how they want to handle as well as express themselves in any particular situation. In this chain, behavior is mainly dependent on a person's thought and emotion. It deals with the cognitive aspect of a person as well as their behavior.

In terms of their train of thought, individuals will learn on how to accept the current situation they're in and, instead of choosing to think about the negative thoughts and emotions, they learn on how to focus more on the positive aspects in life. They try to see the positive aspect in each situation and try to shed light on favorable emotions.

As for the behavioral aspect of CBT, it alters the way that different individuals react to various scenarios. When faced with a problem or situation, CBT allows them to take control of how they might behave and respond to it and lets them be a better person.

There are many different methods and tools of CBT. This type of treatment can be found in health centers wherein professionals can lead you through a rigorous process and help you on your way to wellness.

Some techniques in CBT include the following:

Cognitive Restructuring

Cognitive Restructuring is a frequent CBT exercise that can significantly aid individuals in dealing with their problems. This addresses the way an individual processes their thoughts and ultimately affects the emotions and behavior that follow.

How does it work? Well, CBT is specifically designed to allow individuals to recognize unfavorable thought patterns and find a way to alter them. Through this, it ultimately reconstructs the emotional system and gradually works through a person's depression, anxiety and other emotional and behavioral disorders. It involves identifying all the beliefs and ideas in one's mind and separates the positive from the negative ones.

Next to that, it assesses the unfavorable ideas and tries to turn it into favorable concepts. How? Negative ideas stem from over-thinking or reading too much into a situation. Through Cognitive Restructuring, it finds an unseen benefit under every circumstance and sticks to the positive side of everything. Unfavorable thoughts are eliminated and put to rest by replacing them with positive ideas that can essentially help the individual in the end.

Cognitive Restructuring alters the ideas that a person thinks about when reacting to a situation from negative ones to positive ideas. The way an individual thinks in response to a situation will be turned into favorable ones by identifying unfavorable thought patterns then finding a positive alternative for this.

This can be done in many different ways. First, individuals need to find general and automatic thoughts that are instantly recurring in our everyday experience. Then, we have to assess these thoughts if ever they are actually true and figure out if they are healthy or negative ideas.

Once they have made a decision, the individual has to replace these automatic thoughts with positive ones if ever they are negative in the first place, or keep these thoughts if they are creating good and positive impact in your life. When replacing them, they must create a better and much more favorable point of view that can essentially benefit them. Through this, they can create a good solution to eliminate the item that has been causing them distress.

Mindfulness Meditation

Meditation is practice that allows an individual to attain mental and emotional clarity. This technique uses strategies like mindfulness, breathing exercises, and self-awareness. Meditation can be done in a lot of different ways.

With that being said, there are several known types of meditation, each catering to a specific aspect that can primarily promote a clearer mind and soul. Breath awareness meditation pays attention to mindful breathing. This helps the individual focus more on the way they breathe and disregards all the thoughts that enter their mind. It benefits the individual by minimizing anxiety, worry, greater concentration and a better emotional state.

There are also other types such as Zen Meditation, Transcendental Meditation and Loving-kindness Meditation that can ultimately help individuals arrive at a clearer mind set and better soul.

Focusing more on mindfulness meditation, this particular type of meditation is also recognized to be an effective technique in promoting cognitive behavioral therapy. It can be used as a tool in aiding problems within the cognitive and behavioral aspect. Mindfulness is a type of meditation that coaxes individuals to be aware of the things happening within the present time and become more vigilant of their surroundings. This entirely disregards the past and focuses on the events we have at hand. It dictates that the present surroundings are the only things that matters.

This unique type of meditation can be practiced anywhere, at any time of the day. As an illustration, when individuals are waiting for a long line to purchase something or waiting for the bus at the bus stop, they can easily take note of everything that is currently happening around them. They become more aware of the things that surround them such as the different people, sounds and smell. They perceive what their senses perceive.

Mindfulness can be found in a majority of the meditation techniques. It can be extremely helpful in focusing on different matters. Breath awareness meditation is one example of where mindfulness is also incorporated.

Mindfulness meditation is known to be a great treatment for many psychological problems, ranging from depression to anxiety and PTSDs. The benefits of mindfulness meditation includes lower fixation of unfavorable thoughts and emotions, better focus, sharper memory, reduced impulsive reactions and satisfaction in relationships. Mindfulness meditation can promote CBT because it also alters the way the brain works and how it processes information. It can reduce negative emotions, as what CBT also does, and boost positive ones to take their place. It lessens anxiety and helps us to change the manner we behave in certain situations to make us be better. Through mindfulness meditation, not only will the individual's mental health be enhanced but as well as their physical structure too.

Mindfulness pays closer attention to thoughts and emotions, which are actually the 2 main and crucial aspects of CBT. Since it promotes a positive and desirable outcome for an individual's train of thought, it will most likely result to favorable emotions and better behavior.

Graded/ Gradual Exposure

Another viable technique for Cognitive Behavioral Therapy that individuals may utilize is graded/gradual exposure. This exercise is specially created with the intention of reducing fear and anxiety by slowly and progressively facing them and coming in contact with that object, place, situation or person. Graded/Gradual Exposure is actually perceived to be one of the most common and effective methods to take in overcoming a certain psychological problem. Professionals from all over the world have the same favorable results regarding this treatment and can say that it has really helped multiple individuals around the globe in coming to terms with the things they fear the most.

Therefore, here's the story. Individuals tend to avoid the things they don't want or fear the most. As a result, their fear of that particular object, place, person or situation will only increase as they think about it. However, if they try to expose themselves to that particular fear in a gradual manner, they may be less inclined to fear it. This will slowly reduce their fear for that certain matter until will ultimately disappear.

To better understand it, here's an example. A person who is extremely afraid of being in closed and confined spaces, termed as Claustrophobia, will typically try their best to avoid being put in that certain situation. Through graded/gradual exposure, therapists will try to coax them into facing their fear little by little. Initially by putting them in a large yet close area, then gradually reducing the enclosed space through each session. With this method, they are slowly facing their fear and coming to term with certain facts and realities. At the very end of the treatment, most claustrophobic people would now be able to withstand and curb their fears and are no longer fit to be called claustrophobic.

Graded/Gradual exposure is connected to CBT and may actually promote it since it also does what CBT does. It alters the way that individuals think and how they perceive certain things. With graded/gradual exposure, individuals are faced with their fears and shown what reality is actually like and different alternatives from their perspective.

Graded/gradual exposure also changes the way a person reacts, responds and behaves in a certain situation. It transforms the way they used to react since it is also connected to the way they think. Thoughts are the root of what stems from their behavior. Because it changed their thoughts, it also ultimately made an impact on their behavioral aspect.

In CBT, an individual who has a fear of heights (acrophobia) will have to alter the way they perceive their fear. When placed in a situation that involves heights, they need to alter their negative thoughts and transform these into positive ones. Once this is done, their mind will relax along with their body and act more naturally instead of screaming in fear.

People with this fear are slowly exposed to different height ranges. As they gradually go higher while they progress, they will learn that their fear will slowly disappear. Once it disappears, their mind would have already been altered with favorable as well as positive ideas and their behavior towards the situation would have changed from screaming or panting in anxiety to calm composure.

Activity Scheduling

This is a prominent Cognitive Behavioral therapy technique that is often regarded to be effective and efficient for individuals. This is also known to be very helpful for those who experience or deal with different psychological problems, especially depression.

People who are battling with mental disorders, such as depression, are often finding it tough to stay active and in fact, would then to lay on their bed throughout the entire day. Therefore, in order to avoid being passive the entire time, activity scheduling is one of the many solutions they can use in order to solve their passive state and make an effort to become much more productive for the entire day.

Activity scheduling includes taking a part in different activities and behaviors that they normally wouldn't do as a result of anxiety, depression, and other psychological problems they might be currently facing. It entails a two-step process that can essentially help the individual be a lot better in the end.

Starting off, it begins with monitoring personal activities. Individuals have to take note of their activities throughout the entire week and see the different things they have achieved throughout the course of a week. This can show people that they can actually achieve many things if they put their heart to it. Once the set of activities are listed and made, looking at it will improve the individual's mood when they realize the different things they were actually able to accomplish. Secondly, they would have to rate the intensity of the symptoms of depression they are experiencing alongside each activity. Through this, they can be able to identify the different activities that can actually be more helpful for them and keep their mind off of disturbing or depressive thoughts. If they look more into the pattern of activities that help them become happier and see the connection of each activity, they can devise an itinerary of things that can introduce wellness and possibly cure depression.

It is used to promote CBT since it caters to the way an individual acts in every situation. It monitors their movement and ways of behaving in a certain scenario. Through this, their behavioral aspect can be influenced and aided significantly. Activity scheduling is actually one of the many activities that can help an individual in their CBT journey.

Activity scheduling can be essential in pointing out the different activities that can promote wellness and happiness for an individual. In this process, they are given a specific tool to find out which ones are actually helping them overcome this illness and what makes it worse. Activity scheduling is often used by different therapists to treat depression from all over the world. When used effectively and accurately, it can lead to great results.

Behavioral Activation

Another Cognitive Behavioral Therapy exercise that can be used in treating several psychological disorders is

Behavioral Activation. This technique enables us to get the deeper meaning and connection between a person's thoughts and behaviors. Each aspect significantly affects the other. Thoughts are deemed the root of everything. If a person has negative thoughts running through their mind, they will most likely tend to do negative acts and express negative behavior as well. These factors create a chain reaction with one another, if one aspect is touched or bothered; the other one will most likely follow in its way.

CBT is known to be extremely helpful for aiding different mental disorders. Behavioral Activation is one of the CBT skills that can ultimately help individuals overcome their psychological problems and create a better life for them in the future. Behavioral Activation is also noted by many therapists to be extremely useful in treating depression. It involves a long process that will ultimately lead to a better and fitter state of mind.

This process starts with getting to know your own feelings and coming to terms with the things, you are currently experiencing. Individuals have to understand how they feel, where these emotions come from and what triggers them. Afterwards, they need to take note of the things they typically do on a daily basis. When this is done, they have to find out what they want to get out of life. They should see their goals and objectives. Then, their energy has to be directed towards wellness and motivation to do the things they want and accomplish their objectives. Ultimately, it all depends on having a good and positive change, even if it is little by little just to show progress in their activities.

For a greater understanding about behavioral activation, here's an example of how it's used. A man who deals with anxiety and depression often has different moods throughout the day/ week. There are days wherein he'd feel ecstatic and joyous and some where he feels extremely depressed. Then, when he actually takes note of the different things he has done throughout the day, he would have noticed that there are actually some activities that are considered emotional triggers for him. Since he is aware of the things that might potentially trigger him, he tries his best to stay away from those emotional triggers to keep a calm and collected vibe. He changes the way he acts towards these specific situations, which evidently also would change his mood throughout the entire day. So, in this method he was able to identify the different emotional triggers he includes in his daily routine and was able to find a way to deal with those triggers.

Behavioral Activation is a useful and oft used tool in Cognitive Behavioral Therapy because it also deals with the cognitive and behavioral aspect. It helps a person to understand his/her situation and come to terms with their daily activities, which may be impeding them from leading a good and normal life. It helps them figure out a way to negate their unfavorable thoughts and turn them into positive ones.

<u>Problem Solving</u>

Problem Solving is also another common and notable technique used in Cognitive Behavioral Therapy. In this method, individuals are taught on how to solve their issues, cope with the different problems they are faced with and try to regain better control over their lives. Problem solving uses a unique way in dealing with psychological issues. It directly deals with life's challenges and takes it head on. It immediately faces the problems with the use of cognitive and behavioral interventions.

This method teaches individuals how to have an active role when making decisions for a tough decision. As a result from repeated disappointments or chronic mood problems, some individuals may prefer to take the back seat and get a passive role during tough times. However, problem solving is here to teach individuals that they have to get more initiative and do whatever it takes to arrive at the goal they want.

CHAPTER 4: How CBT Works: Explaining The Mechanisms

The entire purpose of cognitive behavioral therapy is to switch around our way of thinking and the behaviors associated with our thought processes. This method of treatment helps many people solve emotional, social, medical and work related issues by diving into the past to help provide clearer insight into our feelings and why we think and feel the way we do. CBT targets our thoughts and beliefs that we feel right now.

There are specific skills that are involved when recognizing and fixing distorted thinking, modifying beliefs, and how to relate to others in an entirely new way, which helps patients learn to behave in ways that are more desirable.

The point is that negative cognitive perceptions will lead one to unhealthy thoughts and behaviors. When one experiences something stressful, automatic and intrusive ideas come to mind that greatly affect their moods and emotions of the situation. This can cause someone to overact, feel sick, or fret. This is because they are making false assumptions on the meaning of things they experience based on an unreliable truth.

For instance, someone who fears going to the dentist may dwell on the pain they felt from a previous possible dental procedure. This fear is likely triggered by a childhood traumatic event. This can cause them to lose sleep, deal with anxiety, and neglect caring for their teeth altogether.

Cognitive-behavioral therapy alludes to a therapy discipline that includes parts of both behavioral and cognitive therapy. The treatment may consist of an assortment of methodologies and frameworks all intended to accomplish pretty much something very similar: challenge the patient's perspectives (which are twisted and along these lines prompting crippling practices) and help them learn approaches to adapt to stress.

Cognitive-behavioral therapy endeavors to go past the primary method for dealing with stress training of most facilities; specialists are progressively keen on helping the patient overcome their fears as opposed to staying away from dubious circumstances or sedating patients.

What are some usually proposed techniques for CBT? Progressive introduction therapy includes gradually and deliberately presenting the patient to surely understood fears. Orderly desensitization is along a similar vein; however, regularly manages mimicked circumstances and the points of view of the patient.

Different techniques utilized in CBT may include having the patient keep a journal of emotions and occasions, addressing convictions that are nonsensical, and trying different things with new resistance systems, just as various responses to stress. Notwithstanding these techniques, cognitive behavioral therapy may likewise include having the patient keep up unwinding practices and even gain proficiency with some diversion techniques for adapting.

This type of therapy has demonstrated to be extremely effective in treating some character issues, including summed up anxiety issues and social anxiety issues. Some in the medicinal network have even recommended it is unquestionably more effective than pharmacological medications in the long haul.

Cognitive-behavioral therapy is an effective treatment against most kinds of disorders, if drugs or liquor don't adjust the individual's perspective to unnatural levels. This likewise applies to different cases in which outer components have a considerable influence. How Does Cognitive Behavioral Therapy Work?

Cognitive behavioral therapy is a very commonly used form of psychotherapy. This specific form of therapy treatment can sometimes be even more beneficial when it is combined with other types of treatments such as with the use of antidepressants or other prescribed medications. A central focus in cognitive behavioral therapy is to assist people in becoming aware of when they perceive things in a negative manner and to make interpretations of what has happened based on these negative perceptions. In general, patterns of behavior will reinforce the distorted thought processes and thus continue the cycle of distortion. The goal of cognitive behavioral therapy is to break this cycle with the introduction of behavioral changes that the patient will be able to utilize in all future interactions that occur.

Cognitive behavioral therapy is a therapeutic treatment option that aids people in understanding the negative feelings and thoughts and the distorted ways in which they influence their resulting behaviors. It assists people in developing different ways of perceiving situations, achieving different thought processes, and learning different behaviors, which all have an end goal of reducing the overall psychological distress that the person feels. This type of psychotherapy is one that is educative in nature. The patient learns how to observe and analyze his or her own behaviors and how to replace them with more beneficial behaviors that will help him or her to reach their goals. It relies on the person or patient to have an understanding of himself or herself and to have the ability to be his or her own therapist.

Cognitive behavioral therapy works because of the focus on the individual and of his or her knowledge of his or her personal needs and goals. The person or patient needs to have a strong understanding of the disorder he or she possesses, as well as the ability to understand how it affects him or her on a daily basis and the course that the disorder may follow. This includes things such as self-doubt and negative self-talk and the likelihood of potential for relapses in the illness. He or she will also learn about the way in which cognitive behavioral therapy works, the process to follow to complete the therapy successfully, and the cognitive model from which the therapy was originally developed.

The cognitive model is based on the theory that your thoughts influence your feelings and emotions and that through these emotions, they will also influence your behaviors. So, before a person begins cognitive behavioral therapy, he or she perceives a majority of the things that happen in the world around them in a negative manner. He or she begins to have negative thoughts. The negative thoughts lead to negative feelings and then the negative feelings eventually lead to negative behaviors. As the cycle continues, either the person continues to perceive things in a more negative manner than what they are presented with, or the person's behaviors actually do lead to a more negative environment. In either case, this is a cycle that must be broken and the thoughts and behaviors need to be replaced with more suitable responses to meet the given occasion.

Once in cognitive behavioral therapy, the person will learn to recognize the patterns of his or her negative thinking and the emotions and behaviors that his or her thoughts and perceptions will lead him or her to display. He or she will learn how to allow himself or herself to be able to tune out the negative perceptions and thoughts by determining and utilizing new ways of thinking.

A person typically will work with a therapist in order to break the problems down into separate parts that are easier to analyze. The broken-down portions usually consist of thoughts, emotions, physical feelings, and finally, actions or behaviors. Once broken down as such, the smaller portions can be much more easily analyzed. Then the patient can begin the evaluation process. He or she must look at everything, beginning with the thoughts and perceptions to determine if they are accurate and realistic. In most cases, the patient will discover that he or she has been perceiving things in a more negative way than those in which they really occurred Homework is an essential part of completing cognitive behavioral therapy in a traditional clinical setting with a licensed therapist. This is because the patient will generally only see the therapist between two and four times monthly and each session is usually only somewhere between 30 and 60 minutes in length. The new skills that are learned in therapy sessions must be utilized on an everyday basis for the therapy to be successful in the replacement behaviors becoming second nature to the person. In addition, in the long term, these new skills will continue to be utilized by the patient long after the therapy has concluded in order to maintain his or her mental wellness.

Many times, especially when dealing with anxiety or depression, once an unrealistic negative perception enters the mind of the patient, the thoughts and feelings that occur as a result are also unrealistically negative as well. Eventually, with practice, the patient will be able to implement the new patterns of thought processes and behaviors in his or her everyday life until they become automatic and replace the prior more negative thoughts and behaviors.

How CBT Can Help

Now that you've been acquainted with a brief history of CBT and how it has developed and changed throughout the years, it's time to move on to the many different ways CBT can help people. Enumerated below are just a few of its many benefits and advantages, such as:

It can solve a specific problem

This makes CBT an incredibly versatile approach and enables it to address a wide range of issues just by identifying the maladaptive thought or behavior the client would like to correct the most.

It is goal-oriented

It's been said many times that CBT is a goal-oriented therapy. This means that there is a clear and definitive objective in mind that the client and the therapist must define at the start of their relationship. During every session, they will work towards realizing this goal systematically, and both parties understand what it is that they ultimately want to achieve.

This is an advantage because it clarifies the purpose of the therapy and makes sure that both the therapist and the individual agree about what they are looking to achieve. Sometimes, with other kinds of therapy like psychotherapy or behavioral therapy, this is not the case. In CBT, what the client wants to achieve is often what the therapist will do for them.

It gives the client more freedom

Similar to the previous point, another advantage that CBT has over other psychotherapeutic approaches is that it is more collaborative than most. CBT practitioners often work together with their clients to help them overcome their problems and alleviate their psychological distress. It is directive and focused, but it also allows the client more freedom and control over the therapeutic process.

CBT is also more interactive and requires mutual effort from both parties for the therapy to succeed. The therapist's role is to listen and guide them through their thoughts and experiences; while the client needs to be open, honest, and expressive. So while the counselor's guidance is important, the client's participation and involvement is equally as integral..

It deals with current problems

Unlike other therapeutic approaches, CBT mainly deals with present-day problems and experiences. It addresses thoughts and behavioral patterns that are currently detrimental to the client. It does not dig deeper into their past or analyze their childhood experiences and subconscious drives. Rather, it is firmly rooted in the here and now, and it emphasizes the client's current issues at hand.

This is part of the reason why it is the least time-consuming of all the therapeutic approaches, and a factor for why it is so practical and efficient. Clients can start to see positive results and progress quicker because CBT helps them deal with their issues and improve their current state of mind. It doesn't waste time trying too hard to uncover the deeper or hidden meaning behind things.

It is faster than other forms of therapy

This brings us to the next advantage of CBT: it is a time-limited approach. As stated before, it is the least time-consuming of all the kinds of psychotherapy and takes only one to two months before clients can start to see some progress. On average, most clients will often need 20 hourly sessions on a regular basis, usually once a week so that the therapy can be completed in over five to six months.

This is why CBT is the most recommended form of therapy for clients looking for a simple and effective solution that can alleviate their psychological distress and better enable them to deal with their problems. It is quick and efficient, and most people have a good idea about what to expect.

Moreover, clients can also benefit from CBT in the sense that less sessions means it's less costly. It's a great help for people who are seeking professional help and counseling, but cannot afford to spend more than 6 months in therapy (be it due to time constraints or financial reasons).

It is easily accessible

CBT is perhaps the easiest to understand and apply of all the psychotherapeutic approaches. It's highly structured nature lends itself well to several different mediums, which makes it one of the most accessible and widely available forms of counseling. From individual counseling, to group counseling, to self-help books like this one — almost anyone can learn and practice CBT.

It can help with many different mental health problems

An evidence-based therapy, thousands of studies to date have documented and demonstrated the effectiveness of CBT in dealing with a wide range of mental health problems.

From clinical diagnoses like post-traumatic stress disorder (PTSD), generalized anxiety disorder (GAD), social anxiety disorder, borderline personality disorder, and eating disorders like anorexia nervosa and bulimia; to more common problems like overcoming addiction, recovering from substance abuse, dealing with depression, relationship problems, and anger management — CBT can help with quite a number of things, as you can see.

It helps you grow as a person

When you begin to seek help through CBT, it will promote positive behavioral change and personal growth in you. Through this process, you will be able to identify the root of your problems and understand your role in perpetuating your own unhappiness.

CBT can help you see the impact of your negative thoughts and beliefs, and once you do, you will begin to work towards changing them. This will make you more kind, forgiving, and accepting of yourself and your shortcomings, as you will start to correct your own negative self-concepts.

It will make you more positive

Aaron Beck, the founding father of CBT, was able to identify three major kinds of automatic thoughts: negative ideas about the self; negative beliefs about the world; and negative views of the future.

In line with this, CBT is geared towards helping people overcome this negative mindset and instead, encourage them to adopt more beneficial ways of thinking and behaving. In this way, CBT can do a lot to help a person become more positive, as it addresses their negative views of the world and the future.

Cognitive-behavioral therapy (CBT) has the power to transform an individual's way of thinking so that they can replace their negative thought patterns with a more positive outlook on life. Clients will learn to stop jumping to conclusions, stop seeing things as purely all-good or all-bad, stop comparing themselves to others or blaming themselves too harshly for mistakes, and many other different kinds of maladaptive mindsets.

It promotes mental wellness

The main goal of psychotherapy is to promote mental wellness, and CBT is no different. It has countless of different benefits that can do this (many of which we've already named on this list). It can be as effective as medication in treating certain mental health disorders and doesn't put you at risk of dependence or can be helpful in cases where medication alone is not effective.

Other benefits include helping a person reduce their stress, overcome their past trauma, stop over thinking or ruminating, calming their mind, and learning to regulate their emotions better.

The last part has become a focus of many psychotherapeutic efforts of recent years (such as positive psychology and mindfulness). It's important that a person knows how to control their thoughts and emotions instead of letting it control them.

It makes you more rational

In order for CBT to be successful in treating a client's psychological distress or dysfunction, the person must first learn to be aware of their own maladaptive thoughts in order to identify the root of the problem and resolve it correctly. They can do this through mindfulness training, meditation, and practicing emotional self-awareness, all of which helps them to become more objective and reasonable in their thoughts.

Cognitive-Behavioral Therapy (CBT) teaches your mind to see things from a new perspective and consider the truthfulness of your beliefs. It helps you think more clearly and makes you more resilient against negative thinking and feelings, thus allowing for better judgment and decision-making.

It makes you more empathetic

With the previous point in mind, CBT can also help you to become more empathetic by training you to be more level-headed in dealing with your problems. It encourages you to see past your own point of view and helps you see things better from other people's perspectives. You become better at distinguishing facts from irrational thoughts, and you gain more insight into the motivations behind the actions of others.

You can become your own therapist

The last and most important way that CBT can help a person is by training them to become their own therapist. The ultimate goal of CBT is to guide its clients as they overcome their personal dilemmas and teaches them how to change their perceptions for the better, to see things more clearly and constructively.

It shows us how to approach our psychological distress with calmness and peace of mind, which makes us better equipped to handle negative or stressful situations. Moreover, the ability to resolve our problems on our gives us a better sense of control over our lives and builds our self-esteem and feelings of self-efficacy.

Cognitive-Behavioral Therapy (CBT) instills its clients with better coping strategies to help them deal with a wide variety of everyday challenges and overcome the hardships of life on their own. The skills you can acquire in CBT are useful, practical, and helpful in everyday life. It has also been proven to keep people from relapsing into their old, self-destructive ways and improve their overall quality of life.

CHAPTER 5: How to Detect the Underlying Issue

In CBT, the first step is to identify the underlying problem that triggers the harmful and unwanted behavior. This is a crucial part of the therapy as it gives you an area to focus all your effort on.

It is essential to understand that every CBT session should be designed to meet the different needs of each person. There is no blanket rule that will apply in every situation. For that reason, in order to identify the underlying cause for the negative behavior, you must first get a clear picture of how those negative thoughts fit into the entire picture of life.

In the initial visit with the therapist, you will probably be asked a series of questions. One of the first things you and the therapist will work on together is establishing goals. The therapist may not come right out and ask, "What are your goals?" or, "What do you want?" but instead may ask something less obvious, a question that will compel you to think deeply about your answer.

The reason for this is that we are rarely honest with ourselves. The first answer that comes to mind doesn't even address or identify the true nature of our problems. The real answers are often buried deep inside of us, and without some inward severe analysis of ourselves, the true answers may never actually come to the fore.

You could answer this question with the obvious. Many might respond with, "My wife told me to come," or, "I need help," but those answers don't really explain the real reason why you came. Chances are, if your wife told you to come, it is most likely because you are demonstrating certain behaviors, she finds disturbing. This is a good reason for you to sit down and seriously consider why you're seeking out a therapist as that could be the first step in helping you get down to the root of your problem.

How to identify negative thought patterns when they present themselves

Whatever your problem is, you need to identify those tactics you used to handle your behavior, and the odds are high that if you look underneath some strong points you put forward every day, you'll find the root of your problem.

In this period of retrospection, it's vital to take a realistic view of your life and where you're heading. Look closely at how your anxiety and depression are affecting your behavior. Again, you have to start looking below the surface to reveal these behaviors, which may be obvious to other people, but it may not be so apparent to you. Your adverse reaction may appear in different areas of your life.

- Relationships

Some may be struggling with a difficult marriage. However, the underlying problem is not necessarily the marriage but in behaviors demonstrated in the union. If you're depressed, that may present itself as being very irritable, distant, or uninterested. Whether you're talking about a marriage, parent/child relationship, or a friendship, these kinds of behaviors over an extended period of time can really cause damage to a strong bond.

Anxiety also is not easily identified in your relationship. Without knowing how it is affecting you, it can be challenging to see. Neither anxiety nor depression have clear signs that say, "I'm anxious or stressed," or, "This is me being depressed." They are hidden emotions that appear in a myriad of ways that affect your behavior.

You may have lost someone many years ago, friends moved away, lost some jobs, or trust was broken. These things do not have to be recent, as they can be experiences buried deep in your subconscious. However, since they were never addressed, these experiences are resurfacing to damage your present life.

- Career

How you behave at work can reveal many things about yourself. Whether you're a work-at-home mom, or you're a corporate executive, if you have unidentified anxiety and depression, your relationships at work are going to suffer. Are you happy with your work? Do you wake up eager to get started, or do you feel like it is nothing but a tiresome chore, and you feel too unmotivated to perform your tasks?

Some people feel as if they are overworked, others may feel bored, and others may feel unfulfilled. Often, issues with money come up when thinking about work. You may thoroughly enjoy your work but are not satisfied because the money is not enough, or you may be working on a job that you hate because it pays the money you need. Understanding these things will help you identify the underlying problem hidden beneath the surface.

- Well-being

Our physical health can also have an impact on our behavior. Being unhealthy can have a profound effect on our emotions and mental state of mind. Even if we are relatively strong but are not physically active, it can have a strong negative impact on us. If you are dealing with chronic health problems, or you're just too busy to maintain your physical health, it could be the trigger to many of your negative behaviors.

- Drugs and alcohol

Any kind of mood-altering substances can greatly affect your thought processes. If you find that you need to infuse yourself regularly with drugs, alcohol, or any other substance to get through the day, it could be a sign of depression or anxiety. Try to think if any of your family or friends pointed out that you might have a problem. Do you come home every day needing a drink? While you may not be an 'alcoholic,' as some may think, your depression or anxiety may have led you to develop a dependence on these substances in order to cope with the daily stress of life.

- Rest

The body is a highly efficient machine, but it can't run indefinitely. Like all machines, it needs to be refueled, and it needs to rest. If you are not getting enough rest every day or sleeping too much, this can cause problems. Some people naturally wake up the moment the sunrises, while others have to put up a struggle just to wake up. Others may fall asleep quickly but wake up in the middle of the night and cannot fall back to sleep again.

- Relax

Everyone needs downtime from the rigors of daily life. If we have become so busy that we have no time to unwind or enjoy life, our mental state can suffer. Our brains and our bodies need to recharge to stay balanced. Many people who work second jobs to take care of their financial responsibilities or are continually moving from sunrise to sunset so they can manage the necessary things in life, will eventually suffer from anxiety or depression.

If you have no free time or can't find time to slow down and relax, eventually, it will take its toll on you. Even if you have free time, but you can't let your mind relax, you are always thinking of the next task you've got to do, and you can't enjoy your break, this could be a trigger that is causing your negative behavior.

Hopefully, these points have made you look deeper into yourself and your behavior to help you identify the underlying triggers behind your negative behavior. After this type of contemplation, it is the time to set some goals that will help you get your life back on track.

CHAPTER 6: CBT and its influence on

Anxiety And Depression

To get a better understanding of how CBT works, we must get a clearer understanding of how our mind works in general. When we have thoughts, they usually fly through our minds in a tiny fraction of a second; quite often we don't even realize that we've had an idea, let alone the effects it has on our behavior.

So, when you lose a loved one in death, lose your job, deal with a family break-up, or have some other traumatic situation, you are quite likely to feel some level of sadness or even fear about what's in store for your future. These are normal reactions to devastating events in our lives. We don't realize that these feelings and the behaviors that follow are a direct result of our thoughts. Most people will bounce back in time and get back to living life. However, for some, these low emotional states tend to be more intense and can linger for extended periods.

What Is Depression?

Depression, which tends to occur more in women than in men, is the direct result of these lingering thoughts. The way it manifests itself can vary depending on a person's age and gender. In men, it may be seen in symptoms such as tiredness, irritability, and sometimes anger. Men tend to behave more recklessly when they are depressed, which can be seen by their abuse of drugs or alcohol. These behaviors may often be passed off as masculine, so they are less likely to recognize it as depression and are not inclined to seek help or treatment.

Women in a depressed state are more likely to appear sad and have deep feelings of worthlessness and guilt. They may be reluctant to take part in social activities or engage with others, even those who are close to them. Depression in children will also be different. Young children may refuse to go to school or show signs of separation anxiety when parents leave. Teenagers are more likely to be irritable, sulky, and often get into trouble in school. In more extreme cases, you might see signs of an eating disorder or substance abuse.

It is normal to feel low, moody or sad occasionally. However, these emotions occur to some people intensely and for extended periods. In fact, the feelings can last even for years for no apparent reason. That is depression.

Depression affects all aspect of your life. Your physical health and mental health deteriorate. It affects how you feel about yourself and that, in turn, affects all the other aspects of your life.

How to know if you have depression

There are different types of depression that have varied indicators. The types will be discussed later. However, some standard indicators can hint depression.

If you notice that you or someone has been feeling down, sad and miserable for most of the time and the same persists for a period longer than two weeks, then that could be a sign that you or the person in question is depressed. Losing interest in the activities that one used to enjoy before and persistent anxiety are, also, some indicators.

Some of the common symptoms of people who are depressed include:

Behavior

- Losing interest in having a social life
- Failing to complete your required tasks. For instance, a depressed student will suddenly stop gettings school work done and even fail to show up for school
- Withdrawal from friends, family, and people that you were once close to
- Having a concise concentration span

Emotions

- Feeling Sad
- Having guilt
- Being very irritable

- Lack of confidence in what you do
- Generally being unhappy
- Being indecisive
- Feeling disappointed
- Generally being sad

<u>**Physically**</u>

- Being tired and exhausted at all times
- Feeling sick and run down
- Having recurrent muscle pains and headaches
- Experiencing sleeping problems
- Loss of appetite
- A significant change in weight. One can either gain a lot of weight or lose a lot of weight

The Main Causes of Depression

So many factors influence how a person feels and the moods they will experience. While no particular item can be singled out to be the cause of depression, there are several factors that aid its development. Often it is not just one, but a combination of events and personal factors and experiences that lead to depression. Here are some of these factors.

Personal Factors

Personal factors are vast. Here are some common ones

- Family issues

Depression has been found to be like a person's family tree. It can be genetic. This means that if your family and relatives are or have experienced depression in their lives before, you are at a higher risk of experiencing it too. However, coming from a family with a history of depression does not automatically mean that you will be depressed too at some point in your life. The circumstances in your life are probably different from theirs.

- Personality

Your personality, also, influences your chances of experiencing depression. People who have low self-esteem, people who worry a lot, those who are sensitive to criticism, self-critical people and negative people stand a higher chance of being depressed compared to people who are more positive and of higher self-esteem.

- Use of alcohol and drugs

People who use alcohol and other hard drugs are at risk of being depressed, as these substances are associated with depression. In fact, most of the people who experience depression have problems with drug abuse. They often resort to these substances as a way of numbing the pain they feel.

- Life events

According to research, continued difficulties and persistent hardships in life like being in an abusive relationship, long-term isolation, being unemployed for a long time, loneliness and prolonged work stresses increase the chances of a person getting depressed. If you are at risk of depression and a trigger event like losing your job or your relationship failing occurs, you are more likely to fall into depression.

- Organical changes in the brain

The brain controls a person's entire body. If there is an imbalance of the chemicals that affect your emotions in the brain, the mind may fail to effectively regulate your moods and put you at risk of being depressed. The influence of the brain over emotions and thoughts is still an area yet to be fully explored, but it is undoubted that changes in the brain may affect your feelings and your chances of being depressed.

The different Types Of Depression

Just like anxiety, there are different types of depression. The symptom can be minor for some depression types and very severe for other types. These are different types of depression.

Major Depression

This type of depression is, also, called major unipolar depression, clinical depression or major depressive disorder. It is usually characterized by having low mood and energy, lack of interest and pleasure in doing the usual activities that you used to enjoy, among other symptoms. These symptoms occur to a person during most of their das and they last for more than two weeks and affect all areas of a person's life.

Major depression can be melancholic, psychotic and antenatal or postnatal

Psychotic depression

This is the types of depression that leads one to lose touch with the happenings of the real world. They experience psychosis. People with psychotic depression experience hallucinations and/or delusions like believing that someone is constantly watching them or that they are bad. People with this depression can get paranoid and believe that they are the cause of all the bad things that are happening.

Antenatal and Postnatal depression

These affect women. During pregnancy, the chances of women experiencing depression are usually very high. They are even at more risk after giving birth for a period of about a year.

The prenatal depression is often triggered by a combination of factors that makes them pretty complicated. Many women experience baby blues – a condition caused by hormonal changes – in the days that follow the birth of their child. This should not be confused for depression. Depression lasts longer and often affects the relationship the mother has with her baby and everyone in general.

Bipolar disorder

A person with bipolar disorder tends to have periods of mania and periods of depression. They have normal moods in between.

Mania is where the person feels really great. They have high energy, talk really fast and they have little need for sleep. They find it difficult to focus on the tasks they are working on and can feel frustrated and irritated very fast. Sometimes they lose touch with the reality and experience hallucinations of delusions. Other times they are of low energy and exhibit symptoms of depression.

Bipolar depression is mainly linked to the history of one's family. Conflict and stress can be common triggers for extreme reactions.

Cyclothymic disorder

Cyclothymic disorder is somewhat a milder version of bipolar disorder. A person with the cyclothymic disorder will experience chronic mood swings that last longer than 2 years. These mood swings involved periods of depression, hypomania and concise periods of normality. The symptoms last for shorter periods of time are less regular and severe as compared to bipolar disorder.

Dysthymic disorder

The symptoms of dysthymia resemble the symptoms of major depression, only that they are less severe. The difference is that, while they are less severe, they last much longer. A person is said to have dysthymia is they experience the associated symptoms for a period lasting more than two years.

Seasonal affective disorder (SAD)

The seasonal affective disorder is a form of mood disorder that exhibits a seasonal pattern. While the causes of the dysfunction are quite unclear, SAD is hinted to be caused by variations in the exposure to light during the different seasons.

SAD is characterized by periods of mania and depression that last during a particular season and end with the season. The most common one that affects many is the depression that sets in during winter and ends when spring sets in.

A person is diagnosed with the seasonal affective disorder if they have been noted to exhibit symptoms of depression during the same season of a year for several years. The most common symptoms associated with the seasonal affective disorder include the loss of energy, excessive sleeping, overeating with an increased craving for carbohydrates and gaining of weight.

SAD is quite rare and is found in only a few countries the experience significant changes in seasons.

Anxiety and depression are not life-long sentences

While almost everyone is at risk of developing an anxiety disorder or a form of depression, the good news is that they are not permanent. There are no specific ways that have been proven to cure depression. However, there are a number of treatment procedures that you can undergo to get back to your normal self.

The different types of depression and anxiety have different treatment types. Some may be conquered through physical exercises while others may require psychological and medical treatment to overcome. The recovery can a very long and tiring process. However, by being intentional and dedicated, you can overcome anxiety and depression. Some of the things someone can do to ensure they get better and stay better include:

- Learning betters of managing stress
- Cutting back and, possibly, letting the use of alcohol and other drugs
- Maintaining a healthy lifestyle

- Being aware of the anxiety triggers and their associated warning signs
- Getting over your setbacks

Also, it is important to share what you are going through with your close ones. Sometimes just knowing that you are not alone is all the therapy you need to get back on track.

Depression often comes in degrees with several different types that we should be aware of. These different types may have many similarities, but you will also find they each have their own unique symptoms that set them apart.

Persistent depressive disorder (dysthymia)

This is characterized by an overwhelmingly sad mood that is persistently present for the majority of a two-year period (one year for children and adolescents).

The symptoms of a persistent depressive disorder may be the same as that of a major depressive disorder but are generally milder.

There are various kinds of depressive disorders that could be remedied by CBT. The symptoms are often very similar in their degrees of intensity. If you recognize some of these symptoms in yourself or in someone, you know, it is strongly recommended that you seek a professional diagnosis and start treatment as soon as possible, so you can get back to living a normal and productive life.

What Is Anxiety?

Closely associated with depression is anxiety, which can manifest itself in a variety of ways. A mild case of anxiety might be evidenced by the sensation of butterflies in the stomach in anticipation of an important event, concern about meeting deadlines, or nervousness about an anticipated treatment or procedure.

For most people, when anxiety is present, they can just ride it out. It is a normal part of life. However, some types of anxiety are far from the norm. Some anxieties can trigger fears (spiders, snakes, planes, etc.) or phobias that are excessive and irrational fears. Many people have a fear of snakes even though they have never actually encountered one. Others are afraid of dogs even though they have never had a bad experience with one. This type of anxiety easily develops into an anxiety disorder.

To help in differentiating between normal anxiety and an anxiety disorder, first take a close look at the cause of the anxiety. Then look at the instinctive response to that fear. If the behavior is considered realistic, then it is probably 'normal' anxiety. However, if the response is viewed as extreme enough to disrupt normal life, it could be classified as an anxiety disorder.

If you are anxious about getting sick, so you take steps to prevent illness. You may use hand sanitizer, regularly wash your hands, or even avoid shaking hands with people in public places. This is a normal form of anxiety. On the other hand, if your fear of getting sick is so strong that you don't want to leave your home or you are regularly washing and cleaning, you may have an anxiety disorder.

There are many different types of anxiety-related disorders out there, and for your convenience, these disorders have been grouped into three different categories:

- Anxiety disorders
- An excessive fear of a real or perceived threat
- Obsessive-compulsive disorders
- Trauma/stressor-related disorders
- The extreme reaction to a past traumatic or stress-related event

If you suspect you or someone you know has an anxiety disorder and is struggling to overcome the symptoms, CBT is one way to help. This method of assisting patients to identify the thought process that triggers the fear may be the best solution to the problem.

CHAPTER 7: Overcoming Anxiety and Depression

Behavior activation is one of the major goals of cognitive behavioral therapy. Behavioral activation is geared at helping patients indulge in enjoyable activities and improve their problem-solving skills. A major consequence of depression is the loss of interest in activities you once found enjoyable. A depressed person will stop caring about the things they once enjoyed because they consider them unhelpful.

Shunning the things you once enjoyed worsens depression, instead of making things any better. Through behavioral activation, the therapist helps the patient let themselves go, as they indulge in enjoyable activities, and the presence of other people makes it even much more enjoyable. Apart from having fun, behavioral activation is also critical in eliminating obstacles, particularly the mental and emotional obstacles.

A patient should keep track of how this experience affects them. If the projected results are not realized, then the patient is at liberty to explore new ways of achieving the desired effect. To a great extent, the success of CBT depends on the cooperation and enthusiasm of the patient.

Our Actions Affect How We Feel

There is a great correlation between how we act and how we end up feeling. Actions that we deem great bring us joy, whereas actions that we deem inappropriate bring us grief. If we engage in activities that we value, we get rewarded with happiness and contentment. For instance, if you attach a lot of importance to socializing, you will always be in high spirits during social events because you are doing something that you consider valuable.

However, when a person gets depressed, they start losing a taste for the things that they once enjoyed. They stop caring about the things they once loved simply because it won't take away their depression. For instance, if they had been big on socializing, they now withdraw from the social scene and start exhibiting reclusive tendencies.

The worst form of depression leads the affected person into isolation and apathy. Consequently, the person misses opportunities for getting ahead in life or having fun.

Behavioral activation challenges the depressed person to drop their negative attitude and start engaging in the activities they once valued. The more they engage in these activities, hopefully, the faster their sense of pride and self-worth will come back.

Steps of Behavioral Activation:

Step 1: Activity and Mood Monitoring

When a person gets severely depressed, they lose touch with their mood changes. Their moods obviously experience oscillations, but the depressed person perceives everything as dark. Behavioral activation helps the patient keep track of their mood changes. The patient is to write down both the activities that they engage in and then rate their depression. Additionally, they are to watch for changes in moods.

Step 2: Focus on Activities That Improve Moods

With the help of a therapist, a patient is to single out the activities that have elicited a great mood and focus on them. The end goal is to ensure that all negativity is banished, and the first step toward achieving this is to boost the patient's moods.

Step 3: Balance Pleasure and Achievement-Based Activities

Some of the activities you are involved in produce pleasure; for instance, dancing and socializing. But other businesses may not be as pleasurable but will give you a sense of achievement; for instance, attending work or cleaning your apartment. To get the best of both worlds, you have to strike a balance between the activities that give you pleasure and the activities that grant you a sense of achievement.

Step 4: Action before Motivation

The patient must do what is expected of them at all times. If there's an activity in their diary, then they must do it. Depression tends to stop a person from taking any action. However, this is limiting considering that action has to be taken before anxiety and depression are gotten rid of. If the activity proves too challenging, the patient should look for something doable that will still help their agenda of improving their moods and getting rid of their depression.

Step 5: Reward Yourself

If you manage to pull through the activities, then you deserve to reward yourself. Handling depression is akin to getting hold of a hot potato; it is extremely challenging. If you have managed to overcome the voices in your mind discouraging you from performing the mood-boosting activities, give yourself a treat.

Behavioral activation might seem like a simple coping skill, but it can be incredibly challenging to pull through the activities, especially if you lack self-motivation. The following are some tips to lighten the activities found in behavioral activation:

Arrange your activities from easiest to hardest

An anxious or depressed person is not exactly the most self-motivated person. Knowing this, you should rank your list of activities from the easiest to the hardest. You are much more likely to get started on something if it's relatively easy than if it were painful.

Identify Activities that are uniquely important to you and measure progress

For maximum effectiveness, identify only the activities that are important to you, as in this way you will be sufficiently motivated. Finally yet importantly, do not forget to keep a track of the results.

CHAPTER 8: How to Forget Panic and Worry

One of the best, result-driven methods of treating panic attacks is CBT therapy. Through CBT, you focus on the behavioral patterns that might be responsible for the attacks. Your therapist will help you identify the things you are afraid of and face your fears. Once you conquer your fears and learn that nothing bad will happen to you, you can overcome the attacks because the fear that comes with the panic attack becomes less gruesome.

Your therapist can recommend any combination of the following techniques to help in managing panic attacks and disorders:

<u>Cognitive restructuring</u>

This is a process where you learn to embrace your thought patterns that invoke panic attacks and replace them with balanced thought processes. The first step is awareness. Once you are truly aware of your thoughts, you can take a step towards understanding how they affect you and why you need to change them.

Cognitive restructuring helps you reduce the intensity with which you respond to panic attacks and the associated symptoms. Over time, you will also realize a gradual reduction in the duration, intensity, and frequency of your attacks.

Relaxation training

Relaxation training is one of the first steps in panic attack treatment. Someone who has experienced a lot of panic attacks over time conditions their body to tense up in anticipation of pain. If this persists, you become vulnerable to stress, depression, and anxiety. Relaxation training is a process where you learn how to control your breathing, relax your muscles, and other techniques of reducing physiological anxiety. As you learn these training exercises over time, you reduce your exposure risks to panic attacks.

Managing stress

For most people, eliminating or reducing stress agents from their environment is the first step towards managing panic attacks. You can learn simple techniques to help you manage stressful situations with minimal conflict. You can also learn how to get out of a stressful situation without confrontation. These simple things eventually play an important role in managing panic attacks.

Exposure treatment

Through cognitive restructuring, mindfulness, and relaxation training, you learn to be less anxious about panic attacks. It is now easier for you to go through some of the situations that you used to avoid before, without feeling anxious or afraid.

Your therapist will introduce you to some of these situations to see how well you can cope around them. This form of exposure is aimed at helping you confront your fears by purposely challenging yourself while fully aware that you are operating in a safe place and nothing bad can happen to you.

Most people need around twelve CBT sessions for panic attacks, though you can also get by with fewer. If you have underlying complications, like OCD or depression, then you might need more than twelve sessions to manage panic attacks.

CBT has proven effective for panic attacks, more so than prescription medicines. CBT is recommended for panic attacks because the treatment process is shorter and the results are longer lasting compared to the conventional talk therapy sessions. One of the reasons for this is because the things you learn in CBT are techniques that you can perform for the rest of your life. You overwrite new beliefs, thought patterns in your mind, and learn to make them a part of your new reality.

At times, these strategies may feel contradictory. For instance, at one point you might track your panic attacks in order to detect patterns or triggers and reduce their frequency, whereas at another point you may be working on strategies to become more accepting of and comfortable with the panic sensations. Your CBT toolbox will include a number of strategies to help you tackle your difficulty with panic attacks from many different angles. With practice, you will figure out which tools work best for you.

The Best Strategies for Panic

Many different techniques have been shown to reduce anxiety and panic. Some of the core CBT interventions that seem to work best include:

RELAXATION STRATEGIES to help you relax and learn how to breathe in ways that calm you down.

COGNITIVE STRATEGIES that help you catch and correct any faulty or distorted thought patterns.

MINDFULNESS STRATEGIES to help you focus on the present moment, as opposed to your fears about what is coming next.

ACCEPTANCE STRATEGIES that help increase your tolerance for uncomfortable feelings, so your panic and anxiety don't derail your day-to-day life.

EXPOSURE STRATEGIES to help you face and experience the very things you are afraid of in order to, paradoxically, reduce your fears. There are three main types of exposure techniques:

1. Imaginal exposure involves imagining, in detail, experiencing your feared events or situations.
2. In vivo exposure involves putting yourself in real life situations that are scary for you.
3. Interoceptive exposure involves exposure to the feelings of anxiety and panic in your body.

Exposure techniques are highly effective in reducing panic symptoms. In many ways exposure is the easiest treatment protocol to develop and follow, because it's so straightforward. However, this type of treatment plan is often easier said (or written) than done. Because of how scary some exposure techniques can be, it's important to incorporate other therapeutic strategies and concepts in order to help you develop the motivation and skills to follow through with an exposure protocol.

Mindfulness

Mindfulness practices are being increasingly incorporated into psychotherapeutic techniques and appear to be highly effective. Rooted in ancient Eastern techniques, mindfulness strategies have been shown to reduce a wide range of psychological symptoms and disorders, including anxiety, depression, and substance abuse. Mindfulness is often confused with meditation, and although there is some overlap, mindfulness is more of an attitude and daily practice as opposed to a singular activity. Researchers studying the efficacy of mindfulness strategies have focused on isolating the following five facets: observing, describing, acting with awareness, non-reactivity, and non-judging.

Mindfulness can be described as the capacity to maintain awareness of, and a sense of openness to, what is happening around us in the here and now. In contrast to being preoccupied with negative thoughts about our past or worries about our future, mindfulness encourages us to attend to the present moment fully and to view ourselves and the world from a nonjudgmental, compassionate stance. This begins with merely observing and describing what you see, hear, and feel in any situation. With this increased awareness, you are then able to act with more intention.

The non-reactive aspect of mindfulness means that you can learn to observe difficult thoughts such as "I am scared I will have a panic attack if I go on the hike" without being emotionally swept up in the experience. You can observe that you are experiencing a fearful thought without necessarily having an intense emotional reaction that accompanies that thought. The nonjudgmental aspect of mindfulness encourages us to stop using labels like "good" and "bad" to define our experiences, but rather to be and observe simply. When he became more accepting and less judgmental of the physiological anxiety experience, he had less fear about it happening, which in turn decreased the severity of his physiological panic response.

As people develop mindfulness skills, their ability to cope with difficult thoughts and emotions improves, and additionally there is often a decrease in maladaptive behaviors and their consequences. For instance, if someone cannot tolerate feeling lonely, they might engage in a host of behaviors to avoid the feeling, such as excessively drinking alcohol or becoming involved in an unhealthy relationship. The more we can remain open and curious about what we are experiencing, instead of judging it, the more rooted we are in the present moment. When we inhabit the present moment, we are less susceptible to being carried away by the emotional stories we tell about our experiences. As it turns out, this makes experiences like loneliness and fear less painful.

Mindfulness techniques are particularly effective in reducing anxiety due to the emphasis on maintaining a present moment "here-and-now" focus. Because anxiety is often anticipatory in nature, when we remain focused on the present, we are less likely to develop psychological distress related to events or scenarios that have not even happened yet. The next time you begin to feel anxious, start by gently pulling your attention back to the present moment.

Mindful Walking

This walking meditation can be done anywhere, but may be more pleasant to do in relative solitude or outside in nature.

1. Begin with noticing your posture. Try to stand as straight as possible, without feeling tight or clenched.
2. Take a moment to roll your shoulders back in order to loosen them.
3. Take a long deep breath in and exhale slowly.
4. As you begin to walk, notice each movement that you make with your feet. Notice your foot lift, your foot hovering above the ground, and

finally the placement of your foot on the ground.

5. Say (or think) "lift," "carry," "place," as you make each movement.

6. Continue walking slowly in this manner for a few minutes.

7. When you are ready to turn your attention away from your movement, shift your awareness to your surroundings on focus on what do you see, what you hear and what you smell.

With its focus on the present moment, mindfulness may be a well-used tool in your CBT toolbox. You can bring your attention to a single moment—to a single breath—with a thoughtful pause, and with movement; you have it available to you at all times.

How CBT Can Help

Panic attacks occur in those who are depressed or who suffer from different anxiety disorders. If you are having a panic attack, then you must confront what other mental health issues might have caused it. You will not have random panic attacks for no reason.

Anxiety attacks can be easily controlled with CBT. When you use CBT methods to overcome anxiety, they may stop the attacks all together. Even if you do still experience an anxiety attack, then you are going to be better equipped with the tools needed to help resolve the attack after it has happened.

Panic attacks are more complex, but that does not mean they can't be helped with CBT. You won't always be able to pinpoint when you are about to experience a panic attack. They might still be random, even after you have invested time in trying to stop them. You can significantly reduce the effects that come along with panic attacks, however. You will also have a higher level of knowledge needed to alleviate the stress after one happens.

You will need to identify what is causing your panic attacks. Are you experiencing moments of depression that have gone unmanaged? Perhaps you have had bouts of anxiety over long periods? Cognitive Behavioral Therapy treatments require you first to identify the reason for the panic before you can determine how to stop the attacks.

Cognitive Behavioral Therapy will get at the root issue and prepare you with whatever you need in order to overcome these attacks. Rather than just trying to alleviate the side effects, such as with a medication like Valium, CBT will help ensure that your panic attacks are not so bad and that you will be able to prevent them in the future better.

How Panic Attacks Occur

Just like with anxiety and depression, many different types of panic attacks and triggers cause them. What causes panic in one person might not affect a different person.

You might also meet someone who has the exact same patterns of anxiety as you.

Genetics play a large role in panic attacks. If your father had panic attacks, then there is a chance that you will experience them too. If you know that your family has difficulty managing their own mental health, then unfortunately, you may have a higher chance of experiencing panic attacks as well.

Huge changes and life events are also going to be inductive of different types of panic attacks. Those who are getting married or about to have a baby can find that they are more likely to experience a panic attack. If you are moving or perhaps going away to college, there is a good chance that you will be having panic attacks then as well. Your body and mind are trying to sync up with new life changes.

Triggers will usually cause anxiety attacks. You may not be able to identify your triggers, but they are still there, so you have to dig deep to determine what might be inducing your panic.

Specific CBT Treatments for Panic Attacks

If you are in a depressive state or feeling increased anxiety, then you might be able to muster the strength to read a book like this one, write in your journal, or do something else distracting. If you are having a panic attack, however, your body is freezing, and it is difficult to think about anything at all, let alone how to solve your deepest issues.

Mindfulness is going to be your most helpful tool. At the very least, remember to use CBT methods that involve counting and focusing on the present. The easiest thing to do when you are having a panic attack is to breathe and count from one to ten. Breathe in through your nose for ten counts, and then exhale slowly through your mouth for ten.

You need to make sure you are putting an emphasis on counting as well. Regulate your breathing patterns so that they don't cause the panic to continue. When we count, not only does it help sync up everything in our bodies but it also gives us something on which to focus. When counting isn't enough on its own, try spelling out the numbers.

Cognitive Behavioral Therapy will help because it will get at the root issue that has been causing so much anxiety and depression in the first place. You might not even notice your panic attacks are cured until it has been a long time since the last one. When you put the focus on yourself and bettering your overall mental health, it will be a lot easier to reduce panic attacks.

Keeping a Journal

Keeping a journal is going to be helpful in all scenarios, but if you are prone to panic attacks, it should almost be required. By marking down everything that you experience, you can better understand what the root issue of your triggers and attacks might be. Writing down information can sometimes be enough to help significantly reduce feelings of stress and anxiety. You might feel lost with your own thoughts, but when you are given a pen and paper to express them, you will have the chance to rationalize them much more easily.

A journal will allow you to look at everything that happened in your day to determine what might have caused the panic in the first place. It is like looking at a map. When you are on the street, you can't always tell which way is the best to go. When you look at it objectively, from a bird's eye view, you can see the correct path.

You do not always have to write journal entries. Sometimes just keeping quantifiable records will be helpful enough. It can be as simple as jotting down a note like "10:30, meeting with boss, heightened anxiety." Then you might write later, "1:00, watched videos on lunch break, felt very relaxed." You would then be able to see that the stressor is likely your boss.

Curing panic attacks isn't always about curing the panic. Curing panic certainly helps but expressing our panicked emotions can be all it takes in certain situations. At the same time, we also have to remember that those who experience anxiety, depression, or panic attacks are likely more prone to memory loss and not trusting their thoughts. A journal can help you remember better and give you the opportunity to go back and see what actually happened and what you might be exaggerating.

Exposure

Exposure to the things that cause you anxiety is going to be very helpful, but only if you are up for it. If you are afraid of clowns, you can't force yourself to look at clowns until you like them, but some exposure can help alleviate the symptoms that come along with the panic you experience when seeing one.

If you try to expose yourself when you are not prepared, you can actually end up causing more damaging trauma. It is best to make sure that you are doing what you can to reduce trauma around the issue. Don't go in all at once either. Take it systematically and remember that other people are going to have different paces than you.

Exposure therapy is probably best done with a therapist, though you can do it on your own. You might think you are at a point where you are strong enough to handle confronting your issues, but you could also end up sending yourself into a panic from which you cannot recover.

Then you would look at pictures of spiders. They might be small spiders at first, and then each picture you see is of a bigger spider. After that, you might want to watch videos of spiders. When you don't feel the same initial fear after looking at the videos, then you might even try seeing a live one.

You don't have to get to a point where you are holding a spider or keeping them as pets. You just want to get to a place where you don't have a panic attack over the fear of seeing a spider.

Coping Strategies

Sometimes preventing panic attacks isn't a surefire way to guarantee that they will never come. Instead, you might have to come up with coping strategies to use after the attack occurs. Panic attacks are scary, but if you know how to get through them and recover afterward, they won't be so bad. Sometimes the fear of a panic attack is enough to induce one, so preparing for them is enough to alleviate that fear.

Look at the things that keep you the least stressed. Maybe it is a certain location, a poem, a person, or a pet. Whatever it is that calms you down, let it be your mascot. Think of it when you are feeling stressed and use it to reduce your anxiety overall.

Keep a song downloaded on your phone that will help reduce panic when you feel it creeping up. Have a game ready to play, such as Tetris or Sudoku, which will help you take your mind off what is causing you so much panic.

Remember to use healthy coping strategies. Chugging a beer might help reduce your anxiety after a panic attack, but is it really going to help you in the long run? Always look for activities that will help you grow, not just ones that temporarily distract you.

Anger is another of those emotions that is normal in moderation, but when it starts to ramp up or get to the point where it is causing repeated problems in your life, you may want to take a step back and attempt to regulate it somehow. When your anger becomes problematic, people around you may try to avoid you in fear of setting you off or making the situation uncomfortable for everyone involved. When your anger is problematic, you may lose it in public, or even find yourself being arrested when you lose your temper so severely that you end up doing something you regret.

Anger is definitely one of those emotions that need to be regulated in order to ensure that you are not causing more harm than good as you go through your life. Many people tend to struggle with anger, mainly because it is a skill to learn how to cope with it that many people never learn in childhood. When that skill goes unlearned, unfortunately, the result is someone who is wholly incapable of controlling him or herself.

CBT and Anger

Luckily, CBT is once again effective at treating this problem. When you have anger problems, you are absolutely stuck in a loop in which your negative thoughts cause negative feelings, which cause negative behaviors.

Somewhere along the way, your thoughts are causing anger, and because you are feeling angry, you are largely going to behave angrily.

CBT seeks to interrupt that negative feeling by interrupting the negative thoughts that cause that anger. This means that, just like how you would treat everything else, through identifying the core value that is problematic, challenging that negative core belief, and then engaging in cognitive restructuring for anxiety, you will go through those steps for your anger as well. In doing so, you are essentially assuring yourself that you can, in fact, take over your anger with the right mindset, and you enter that mindset.

Anger and Fear

What is interesting about fear, however, is that while it is an emotion that has a very specific purpose, in this case, in being able to defend yourself when you feel wronged, threatened, or otherwise in danger, it is a secondary emotion. That means that in order to feel anger, you must first feel some sort of fear. The two are intrinsically combined, with fear coming first and the anger coming as your reaction to the fear in the first place. Think of this as the process in the fight-or-flight response—your anger is the method your body picked to cope with the fear. Your body entered the fight mode and has decided to get defensive.

You may have feared being actually hurt or threatened, or you may have feared being wronged, challenged, betrayed, or even feared losing something. No matter what the fear you had, it resulted in anger, and that anger needs to be dealt with. Because of that, most of the time, your angry core beliefs are actually scared core beliefs or anxious core beliefs. This means that the way you would manage your anger, then, is essentially identical to how you would manage your anxiety. In doing so, you are able to manage yourself better.

Treating Anger

The most effective way to manage your anger with CBT is to eliminate the angry tendencies from your default actions. Instead of automatically defaulting to angry behavior, you need to learn to prioritize instead correcting language. Those who are angry, anxious, and depressed frequently engage in black and white, or absolutist terms. When you are angry, you will think about how you always see a specific reaction, or that you are never able to get what you want or need.

The best way to do this is to engage in the so-called "Socratic questions", which require answers that are in the grey areas rather than considering only the "black and white" options. They force you to begin to consider the nuances between always and never, recognizing that sometimes is a possibility that is just as legitimate, if not more so than always, or never. You can start with questions such as:

- Is it possible to be offended if the other person did not intend to offend you?
- Is it possible to make mistakes even if you are an expert at the thing you are doing at that moment?

Notice how none of these questions have absolute answers. Each forces the individual out of the negative, black and white thinking, and that can sometimes be enough to settle down the anger. You may begin to see that your absolutes are not the only options for thinking, and you may begin to consider the perspective of the other person that has angered you just by recognizing that he or she has a perspective that differs from you.

Managing stress with CBT

CBT enables you to learn and appreciate a better perspective of the situation you are struggling with, learn how to take back control, and reduce the emotional and physiological trauma you experience. Through CBT, you will learn how to manage stressful situations confidently.

Why should you choose CBT to cope with stress? CBT is ideal because you will learn how to identify the specific instances that subdue you under stress. When you know the things that cause you excessive stress, then you can avoid them or learn how to deal with them better.

Some situations manifest in a pattern and form a trend. CBT teaches you how to identify these thought and behavioral patterns that hold you back and keep you from progressing. You will also learn better ways of thinking that will help you get rid of some of the common stress factors in your life and teach you how to cope with situations that you cannot avoid.

Most people struggle with stress because they believe they cannot handle things on their own. This defeatist mentality can affix in your mind and prevent you from reaching your potential. Through CBT, your therapist can teach you how to empower yourself and boost your confidence to deal with such situations in life.

How CBT works for stress relief

In your initial meeting with the therapist, they will try to help you identify and understand thought patterns and recognize that they increase your stress level. You will also learn how to cultivate a different way of thinking that can help you identify stress triggers before you are caught unawares. Over time, you will feel at ease, confident, and composed enough to manage most if not all of the situations that stress you in life.

Your therapist might pose some questions to you about your current predicament. This is to give them clarity about the challenges you are dealing with. This also helps them formulate an action plan to help you manage the stressors effectively.

You will note improvements from one session to the next, especially when you learn how to inculcate a different perspective of each event that triggers stress in your environment. Your reactions to such events can either ease the problem or make it worse. You will first learn and understand why you react or respond to such events the way you do, and from there learn a different approach that reduces stress and allows you to cope better under duress.

There are different issues that arise when you are stressed, which can be treated through CBT. Stress affects your confidence and can make you feel powerless, even in situations that you should exercise control over. Some of the common instances where stress can affect your performance include the following:

- Business or career management
- Managing conflict in your personal relationships
- Depression and anxiety from stress
- Drastic life changes
- Traumatic experiences
- Social anxiety
- Loneliness
- Strained family relations

Most time-conscious people will often ask about CBT: How long it will take me to feel better? Nevertheless, it is not easy to tell how long it will take you to manage stress effectively. Many factors combine to determine the duration of therapy you need.

Your level of self-esteem and confidence is one such factor. Someone who is at the point where they no longer believe in their innate abilities might take a longer time to overcome stress than one who is relatively more confident in themselves.

If you have struggled with stress for a very long time, it might take you much longer to overcome it than someone who sought help earlier. The reason behind this is that the thought patterns and behaviors that you acquire over time eventually manifest and become your comfort zone. This becomes your new normal. Getting you from that point to accept a new reality might take a while, depending on how embedded the traits are in your mind.

Another factor that determines the duration of your therapy is the intensity of stress you are going through. Sudden traumatic experiences might take a longer time to overcome compared to someone who is struggling with simple, work-related stress. It gets worse if, in the course of the trauma, you lost someone close or dear to you.

CBT can be administered in the three categories below:

- 4 to 8 sessions

This is prescribed for someone who is confident in his or her abilities and the situation you are dealing with is not very complicated. It is ideal for conditions that are not prolonged. If you have a high-intensity project you are working on at the office, these sessions can help you regain focus and keep working on it to fruition.

- 10-20 sessions

These sessions are recommended for someone who is dealing with more than one cause of stress. It is ideal for someone who is struggling to cope with things other than the main issue that is stressing them.

- 20+ sessions

If you have struggled with stress for a very long time, then you will need more sessions. This especially happens when you have reached a point of no return. The issues that stress you might be very deep you might have struggled with them for years.

Possible challenges

While CBT has been recommended to help in managing stress and has worked well for a lot of people, you must go in with an open mind. There is a possibility that it might not work for you. Some people quip that some of the symptoms returned after a while or that the process just was not right for them.

Generally, CBT barely treats stress when the underlying cause is deeper or has be\en engrained in your mind for years. This might impede your ability to manage stress. However, you should not give up. Speak to your therapist about the progress you are making. Mention even the slightest changes you notice in your life once you start therapy. In some cases, they can recommend additional psychotherapies to help you cope with stress better. Recognizing the small victories you make will go a long way in encouraging you to keep working towards becoming better.

Cognitive Behavioral Therapy techniques can be used both in the context of therapy and in everyday life. Either way, it's a win. The following techniques are designed to help you overcome your stress.

- Journaling

This technique might seem simple, but it is actually very useful. It is all about writing down your experiences, emotions, and thoughts. Whenever you find yourself struggling with stress, take your diary and write down various things about your condition. Writing down your thoughts not only helps you calm down, but it gives you a new perspective. If you have been stressed throughout the most part of the day, take out your diary and write down the various triggers for your stress. Maybe it was your boss or your colleagues. Write down how you felt about it. In addition, if you have any solution, write it down too.

Unravel your flawed perceptions

Sometimes we get stressed unnecessarily. This usually comes about because of believing something that is not true. Assuming that you're looking for work, and one of your core beliefs is that you are stupid, every rejection letter that you get will cement your flawed belief. If you go around thinking that you're silly, you will develop self-inhibiting tendencies, and you will have a hard time accomplishing your goals.

Expose yourself to your fears

One thing about human beings is that there's no limit to how powerful you can be. You are literally as powerful as you want to be. If you are an introvert, you can very well learn to be around extroverts, as long as you put in the effort. Learn to overcome your stress but putting yourself in challenging situations.

Progressive muscle relaxation

This technique is aimed at making you feel more relaxed. It involves relaxing one muscle group at a time until your whole body attains a state of relaxation. If you're not skilled in this, there are very many resources to help you, especially on YouTube. Whenever you feel stressed, look for a quiet place, put on some soothing music, and get started relaxing your muscles.

Deep breathing

Did you know that you can overcome your stress by drawing in deep breaths? When you draw in a lungful of breath, you are putting more oxygen into the body. And with more oxygen, the brain gets more fuel, which aids in formulating a solution. So, whenever you find yourself being stressed, stop whatever you're doing, and start drawing in and out deep breaths. It will leave you feeling relaxed and free of stress.

CBT for anger

One of the first things your therapist does when you visit them for anger management is to try and help you identify the type of anger you portray. They will also help you understand your thought process to identify a pattern in your anger outbursts. Once you identify the unconstructive traits, you work on a process of changing these habits to a more constructive behavior pattern.

You will learn that most people who suffer angry outbursts struggle to communicate their thoughts, feelings, and needs with the people they interact with. Because of this, they feel no one understands them, and they throw a fit to show their disapproval.

You must also realize that anger is not a bad thing. It is a sign of disapproval that is a normal part of life. However, what you need to manage is the way you express anger. If this gets out of control, you might risk a legal consequence.

Consider your options

The first thing you must remember when dealing with anger is that you have a choice. You might not have control over what someone thinks or does, but you have control over your responses. You can choose if you respond to someone and how.

Often, when you stay quiet and let the situation pass, you enjoy a moment of clarity later. You realize in retrospect that if you would have responded to the situation when it happened, things might have spiraled out of control.

Instead of responding when someone provokes you, take a step back and take deep breaths. Focus on your breathing patterns as you would when meditating. Envision the air gliding in and out of your body. This simple technique eases your mind and helps you avoid an unnecessary confrontation.

While working on CBT techniques to manage anger, you must keep an open mind. Remember that nothing is ironclad in behavioral science. There is always a possibility of setbacks or a relapse. This should not stop you from pursuing your goal. Mistakes happen. Emotional confrontations can catch you off guard Perhaps you find yourself in a confrontation after a night out, and because of the liquor in your system, your rational function is limited. Realigning behaviors and thoughts is a long-term commitment that will only yield results if you stick to your plan and never give up.

CHAPTER 10: Being Mindfulness

As you can imagine, embracing positivity in everyday life can make a profound change in how happy and peaceful your overall life is. When you utilize a positive mindset every day, you will find that life, in general, tends to flow and unfold with more ease and that people in your life then start to respond back to you in ways that are more positive.

I am sure you are aware of this, which is one of the main reasons you are here in the first place! However, the real power is behind actually doing it, not just talking and reading about this positive picture. Trust me, I know the struggle of everyday life, and that it can be a lot to handle. Even during amazing experiences and opportunities, the chaos and demanding challenges of life seem to overshadow the greatness you do have.

While motivating yourself to maintain positivity every single day is not easy, it is more than possible and certainly worth the effort.

First, positive people are usually positive, no matter what, because of two key things:

They practice being optimistic to strengthen this capability further.

They choose to be positive because it feels a heck of a lot better than drowning in a pool of negativity.

We are not born positive or negative, and one person is not more capable of optimism from the next. Stop making excuses about your skills, challenges, or situations you are enduring when it comes to your level of confidence. There are no aspects that make positivity easy, even though many see it this way.

Positivity is primarily a choice. You need both free will and awareness to succeed and maintain a good sense of optimism in your life. Every person, even you, is wired with free will and conscious awareness! You are always in a good place to be more positive and start reaping the benefits from it.

When you are aware of yourself and your life, you will then notice when you are starting to venture down the path of negativity. Having this awareness jumpstarts the choice between optimism and pessimism. Below are some awesome tips you can begin to practice to gain optimum results!

Mindfulness-based Cognitive Therapy focuses on cognitive therapy and mindfulness, rather than the behavioral aspect that we get from CBT. It looks at attitudes and mood which is why it works well for people who find themselves in severe depressive states and suffer from unhappiness regularly. Breathing and meditation is a key component of this therapy.

Mindfulness is about self-awareness in the same way that CBT is, and although CBT is hugely tailored around mindfulness, it does involve some aspects of analyzing and working on those things too, which sometimes means we judge our thoughts and feelings. CBT also focuses on the behavior aspect too and evokes change, whereas mindfulness raises awareness and believes that becoming aware itself can implement the change without forcing it. Both concepts focus on the present and try to implement changes moving forward. By adding mindfulness to cognitive therapy, we demonstrate an appreciation for ourselves as well as showing flexibility in our thoughts.

Important ideas in Mindfulness-based Cognitive Therapy

Mindfulness-based Cognitive Therapy focuses on emotions, thoughts and attitudes. Important ideas in relation to MBCT are:

- Building up a tolerance or coping mechanism that allows us to deal with painful situations better.
- Being open and non-judgmental.
- Reaching an enhanced state of awareness.
- Allowing us to gain insight into ourselves and being in touch with how we feel.
- Using meditation techniques to reflect, recover and cope with specific situations. This can promote emotional wellness.

- Incorporating breathing techniques to help us calm down and cope with our feelings and emotions.

Mindfulness-based Cognitive Therapy is aimed at those that suffer from heightened depression regularly and its key components teach clients to make a break from those negative thought patterns and cope better, whilst improving self-awareness.

How does MBCT Work?

The aim of MBCT is to try and prevent relapses of depression. If a person suffers from regular depressive episodes, it's important to try and change this pattern. MBCT focuses on changing your relationship with your emotions. Mindfulness activities, such as meditation can help to create balance and just like CBT, you can start to change your automatic negative thought patterns and replace them with new ones.

MBCT is about creating a routine and adopting mindfulness technique to cope with an overwhelming situation. The hope is that you can replace your negative thought patterns and prevent those feelings of sadness from turning into depression.

Problems that may be addressed by MBCT

Much like CBT, mindfulness-based cognitive therapy is mainly used when treating depression and this includes moods and feelings of sadness It has been recognized to help those suffering from anxiety disorders, relationship issues, pain, stress and substance misuse too. Let's not forget how useful these coping strategies are in relation to panic too.

If you start to feel down, overwhelmed, or you feel a panic attack coming on, the techniques involved in this treatment can actually prevent it from escalating into depression, although this type of therapy is usually suggested under a therapist if you suffer from depressive episodes regularly (usually three episodes or more).

MBCT Techniques and Exercises

Below are some different techniques and exercises that you might want to explore as part of your MBCT routine. Remember, routine is everything, so planning in time to breathe, meditate, or exercise is a great way to start your MBCT treatment.

Breathing Exercises – Before you can meditate, you need to master your breathing. When we breathe, we typically use our chest and we raise it up and down as we inhale and exhale. Breathing from the diaphragm and stomach area is recommended with MBCT and this involves relaxing your stomach and allowing it to rise and fall as you breathe deeply. You may need to practice your breathing, daily, so spend some quiet time focusing on your breathing technique. You can lay back in the chair, close or open your eyes, or you may prefer to lie down.

Guided Meditations – Many people learn to get themselves into a meditative state without being conducted, but for beginners, there are many guided meditations you can use online, on channels like Youtube. Often, guided meditations focus on a specific area, but there are ones that focus on sadness and depression. If you're going to try guided meditation, research the different ones available and listen to them for a few seconds until you a find soothing voice. Once you've found the one for you, kickback and relax. You should practice your breathing techniques for a couple of minutes, just before you begin.

Walking Meditation – With any meditation, you need something to focus on and in this case, you focus on your walking. You don't focus on each step or look at your feet, you simply focus on the fact that you are walking. Walking is a great way to clear your mind and because it's exercise, it gives you the opportunity to refocus, and you will feel refreshed.

Yoga Stretches – Yoga is an excellent exercise for mindfulness, CBT, and MBCT as it is already a meditative exercise. There are different types of yoga, and some are more spiritual than others. Kundalini Yoga is meditation based and involves quite a lot of breathing exercises as well as chanting. You can attend a class, or there are tutorials online too, if you would prefer.

Other techniques from CBT like journaling, are helpful for MBCT. Recording your thoughts shows that you're paying attention to yourself and your needs. It's a form of self-care which we could all do with a little more of.

Benefits of Mindfulness

As mentioned already, being mindful is a way to take care of yourself and this has numerous benefits for your mind and body. This includes:

- Better general health and state of mind.
- Improved concentration levels.
- Insight into one's self and more in tune with emotions.
- Better control of thoughts and the ability to reason.
- Stronger problem-solving skills.
- Feeling motivated and positive.
- Decreased stress and anxiety.

Mindfulness Skills

Being mindful helps us to embed many skills that can help us in our life. It can help us to process our thoughts in a more positive way, as maintaining a fit and healthy outlook. As we feel happier and healthier, we take back control of our lives and we are less likely to feel depressed, anxious or stressed.

Mindfulness can help us to appreciate ourselves and understand the importance of caring for our mind and body. When we feel motivated and content, we are able to overcome barriers that hold us back. We can also feel rested and relaxed which helps us to reason.

This means that we often live for the moment and live a happy, fulfilling life!

Other Alternative Cognitive Behavioral Approaches

There are several alternative cognitive behavioral approaches that you can consider: Acceptance & Commitment Therapy - ACT is different to CBT because rather than challenging negative thoughts, it encourages you to accept your ideas and then you use something called diffusion techniques to help you overcome these thoughts. You use three broad categories of methods, the first being acceptance, the second is mindfulness, and the third is based on your commitment to your values. Values give us a purpose, allowing us to reflect on what is really important to us in life.

With this type of therapy, you can still set goals to move forward and it's suggested that knowing our values can free you from the stresses in your life.

Dialectical Behavioral Therapy - The main goal of Dialectical Behavioral Therapy is to gain balance as you expose yourself to difficult emotions by recognizing and experiencing them, then you aim to make a positive change to your behavior.

This therapy is closely linked to CBT as you still set goals and it's aimed at people who feel intense emotions and react in a damaging way. The most important thing is to accept yourself and your reactions, and then try to change these negative or harmful behaviors

By talking with a therapist, you can gain an understanding of why you feel and act the way you do, which is part of the acceptance process. It's only when you've taken the first step of 'acceptance', that you then become ready to make those positive changes and move forward

Metacognitive Therapy - Metacognitive therapy was initially designed to treat generalized anxiety disorders. This refers to metacognitions, which are claimed to be the aspect of cognitions that actually control our thinking process. They refer to negative thinking patterns as being Cognitive Attentional Syndrome and they are driven by underlying positive or negative beliefs. The therapy then focuses on challenging and removing the negative beliefs. It can help you gain control of your thoughts by raising awareness and it helps you to cope with negative ideas and thinking patterns.

We can be trained to use our metacognitions to retrieve our memories, but they generally operate in the background. By the end of the metacognitive treatment, you can have a more flexible response.

There are many different types of therapies, techniques, and treatments when it comes to Cognitive Behavioral Therapy and we've also explored related therapies too. The most important thing is finding an effective treatment or therapy that suits your needs and symptoms. Sometimes, you may wish to try different techniques until you find the one that fits you best.

Once you find the right treatments, techniques or therapies, and you start to make progress, you need to start thinking about integrating CBT into your daily life and maintaining the momentum to ensure you don't slip back into your own ways

 Many people find that in the initial stages of CBT, they need some assistance with the practices and therapies. Sometimes, they even hit a roadblock when they've made some progress. There's no right or wrong time to change your CBT therapy or treatment. Again, this is individual to you, and your needs.

CHAPTER 11: Reset the Attitude Toward Life

There is power in positivity that goes more than what meets the eye. You can indeed make a difference in your outlook when you look on the bright side of things. You will wake up in the morning on Monday thinking: "I can do this! I want to go to work today! It's going to be great!"

When you see that you can bring something good into this world, you will need to have a positive attitude and adjust your expectations. Think about it. Life is too short for you to go through it while complaining about every little detail. And we know that everyone likes to complain about the little things in life, such as a meal that is taking too long to be prepared in a restaurant, the noise that's happening during your coffee break or the temperature in your office. Although life is a bit of a downer sometimes, it does not always need to be like that. For this reason, we are going to look at how you can have a positive attitude and how it can change the way you approach new situations.

First, it is essential to realize that there are a lot of sources of difficulties and challenges in our lives. Nothing worth pursuing ever comes easily. It always takes hard work and dedication to accomplish even the most minute of tasks. And often, we cannot achieve our goals because we are discouraged under the weight of all the expectations that have been cast on our shoulders both by others and ourselves. In the midst of all of that, there is a need to pursue our goals and dreams. When we think about the end goal, then we know that we are always moving forward, one step closer to that milestone that will make a difference in our lives. Perhaps your goal is earning that extra $5,000 per year or putting aside money for your next vacation or becoming healthier and having a more positive outlook and overcoming your depression. Sometimes, the more straightforward goals are better because they can lead us to pursue the more involved ones.

Want to Be More Positive? Practice Gratitude

So, you might ask, "Tina, how do you get this positive mindset that is supposed to change my life?" Well, I can say that it is a lot easier for you to achieve that than you may think. What I want you to do right now is write down ten things that you are thankful for on a piece of paper. Get out a pen and notepad, and jot down all of your thoughts. Give yourself about five minutes to do this. You can see what influences your thoughts by getting a feel or what makes you thankful.

Gratitude is one of those powerful things. It helps you get out of the rut whenever you feel stuck. It makes you happier. It enables you to overcome the depressive blues. When you have a situation when you lose a job or have a catastrophic situation throw you a curveball, you may feel helpless and completely shattered from the damage that it has caused you. However, when you write down what you are thankful for, you will see how much blessed you are and have been given much in your life. The truth is, no one deserves this life. It is a gift - and a precious one at that. When you realize how much stuff has been handed to you, you should see that you have many people to thank for pulling you out of the gutter. Think of your parents, friends, financial situation (whether it's good or bad), community, job (not everyone has a good job these days), et cetera. Reflect on these blessings and take away the feelings of entitlement which you may be feeling about them. Realize that you get a lot more than what you deserve, and that is a gift of grace. Taking a moment to say thank you to someone who has made a difference in your life is an integral part of practicing gratitude. And, believe me, it will light up your whole day.

Stop for a Minute and Write Down Ten Things You are Thankful for and Then Come Back to Me

After doing that, you are on your way to becoming a more positive person. Remember a time when you were successful. In high school, you got an A on that English paper and ended up getting a good grade in the class. Or, in the university, you landed a premium internship for a consultancy firm that eventually led to a full-time job there. Perhaps you were able to overcome a severe disease that you got healed from miraculously. Be grateful and remember the times that went by and how you managed to get over many things. Think of how strong you are in surmounting any challenge that comes your way. Not everyone can fight as hard as you can. Having a mental illness can be hard. It can be so debilitatingly difficult to get out of bed in the morning. As soon as you have been able to overcome that difficulty, recognize it and celebrate it! It's the best way forward!

Helping is a form of therapy, which enables you to make a difference with others around you. When you have a mindset of helpfulness and positivity, you can change a lot of things everywhere, as well as develop your mindset and attitude. For instance, if you smile at your reflection in the mirror and at others, you will find that you feel a lot better about yourself. It will allow you to feel much better about yourself. It will enable you to enjoy that positive emotion.

This effect can be more powerful when you try laughing. Whether you crack a joke, watch a comedy on Netflix or laugh with your friends, laughter has been proven to be a great medicine to fight off the negative thoughts that may surround you. All of these things contribute to your positive feelings and enable you to feel excellent in the process. It is crucial to develop a mindset of playfulness, gladness, and thankfulness. This will make you a positive hero who can be a source of light amid the darkness of negativity in this world. As we have mentioned, there is much to be depressed about in this world; however, you can do your part to make the planet a better place by infusing your environment with positivity. That is going to change both your mindset and the world itself.

I am not going to lie to you; it is going to be hard to be positive at times. You might suffer a lot from the cares and worries of this life. Some days, you may wonder, "Why do I care? Why should I go to work today?" You may want to lay in bed all day and sleep because you cannot motivate yourself to keep going. But what if I were to tell you that it is possible to overcome your self-doubt by being a positive and more productive person? Indeed, it is possible.

Be your positive hero and do that for others. That is a solution that is going to make a difference in this world. The way forward is to be the best person you can be, and that means playing on your strengths and developing your weaknesses. As we saw with the example above, Jeremy was able to get over his weakness by getting a "C" in his math class successfully. He did that with hard work and dedication but also with the help of his mentor and tutor, Jack. Together, they were able to accomplish the impossible, and it was amazing how it happened.

That is something you can achieve as well. Practice positive thinking, and you'll see the result of your hard labor and devotion. You have to work at re-shaping your attitude into something that you can do for yourself. It takes dedication and commitment and will involve your reshaping your mindset - that is true. However, when you give it your all, you will realize that everything is possible and that you can achieve your dreams when you set out to do so. When you believe in yourself, anything can happen. You can climb the highest mountain in the world, for one. You can get an "A" on the test that you have been dreading to take. You can achieve a Master's or even a doctoral degree. You can travel the world. You can be the person you were designed to be.

Believe in yourself and you will get to your dreams. Then, you can live a healthier, happier, and more meaningful life.

Epilogue

If you have made it to the end of this book, you can be satisfied with yourself, as it is no small feat, especially if you were completing all of the steps and activities as you went along. This book crammed a lot into a short period in an effort to be as efficient and helpful as possible without being long-winded. Within these pages, you have discovered all of the key facets of completing cognitive behavioral therapy on your own without the need to seek a counselor.

During the course of reading this book, you were provided with the most important information to understanding what anxiety entails. You were provided with symptoms and common disorders, as well as a multitude of ways that anxiety can affect your life. From there, you were given all of the background information on cognitive behavioral therapy that you would need to complete the rest of this book successfully.

You were guided, systematically, through a process of cognitive restructuring. You began by learning how to identify thoughts that would need extra attention. You were also taught how to identify your emotional triggers. With all of the background information you needed on how to identify areas of your mind that needed restructuring, you were given the tools to begin challenging your negative thoughts, cognitive distortions, and your triggers. You were also given ways to begin the cognitive restructuring process, which allowed you to begin inserting positive thoughts in to replace the negative. Lastly, you were given some last-minute skills that would aid you in real life when you try to implement all of the changes on your own.

Hopefully, between the activities that this book provided you, and the concise, yet comprehensive information you were given, you will begin to feel a noticeable improvement in your symptoms of anxiety or frequency of your anxiety attacks. Remember that this is a long, arduous journey, and it will take plenty of time, effort, and of course, missteps before you achieve the results you want. If it were easy to restructure your thoughts and banish anxiety, you would not be reading this book right now.

One last time, because this is so important to reiterate, if you feel as though your anxiety is unmanageable, even with the tools this book has provided you, please seek the advice of a medical professional. This book is not a substitute for medical advice or a medical professional and is meant to be a reference for yourself as opposed to a cure-all for anxiety. Remember that every person is different and has different needs, and if this book is not meeting the needs you have, there is no shame in moving on to another book, approach, or choosing to seek the guidance of a therapist to help you through this tough time. No matter how you choose to do it, know that you have the strength within you to alleviate your symptoms. You can, and will, manage your anxiety.

As you go off on your journey toward mental wellness, try to remember the key components this book advised. Seek to use your affirmations regularly, set SMART goals, and remember how to ground yourself when you are feeling emotionally volatile. Remind yourself that you can do this, and even when you feel like it is impossible, remind yourself that you are capable of doing it. You will just need to find the right toolset that works for you. Good luck on your journey to managing your anxiety, and I sincerely hope this book will be a valuable resource in that journey.

9 781801 255370